A scientific, philosophical, and spiritual excursion
into the true nature of reality and our place in it.

CLOUDLESS REALITY

For anyone looking for answers to life's big questions

Pete Rawlinson

©Pete Rawlinson 2023

The moral rights of the author have been asserted.

All rights reserved. No part of this book may be reproduced by any mechanical, photographic, or electronic process, or in any form of a photographic recording, nor may it be stored in a retrieval system, transmitted, or otherwise copied for public or private use, other than for "fair use" as brief quotations embodied in articles and reviews, without prior written permission of the copyright holder.

A catalogue record for this book is available from the Library of Congress.

www.cloudlessreality.com

*To see a world in a
grain of sand
And heaven in a wildflower,
Hold infinity in the palm of your hand
And eternity in an hour*
~ William Blake

To my very patient partner in life, Fiona,
to an inspiring daughter Saoirse,
and to a snoring pug Sadie!

Thank you

Contents

Preface xii

Introduction 1
What's It All About?
Searching for Why We Feel Unfulfilled 3

Chapter 1 6
Imaginary Me
Why Do We Feel Unfulfilled? What's Missing? 6
Masking Reality 6
Imaginary Me 8
It's Not Real 11
From Prunes to iPads 13
Building an Imaginary Me 22
The Emotion Store 24
Dissolving the Illusion 28

Chapter 2 30
Getting Perspective
What Is Your Current View of Reality? 30
Defining the Real World 30
Self-Protection Mode 33
The Gift of Introspection 34
Much Ado Over a Chip 38
It's All About Me 40
Time and the Imaginary Me 45
How Do We Perceive Physical Objects? 51

A Hard Problem 52
Understanding What Things Are 55
The Vicious Cycle 58
Distortions of the Illusory Self 60

Chapter 3 62
The Human Experience
Is Reality Just One Big Experience? 62
Perceiving Reality Through Direct Experience 62
Are Objects Real? 63
Meeting the Observer 73
A Cloudless Sky 80
Managing Clouds 83
Changing Perspectives 86

Chapter 4 87
Life in the Whirlpool
So What Does Reality Really Look Like? 87
Pure Awareness 87
No Physical Matter 91
The Dreamworld of the Higher Mind 92
Whirlpools in the River 95
Going with the Flow 97
Physical Laws 101
Self-Realization and Meaning 102
On Purpose 104
Our Role and Purpose 107

Chapter 5 109
Fundamental Concepts
**What Does This Mean for Time,
Interconnection, and Free Will?**... 109
What Time Is It, Really? 110
Reducing Time 113
One Present Moment 117
Interconnected All the Way Down................................. 119
Who's in Charge Here?.. 124
The Actor's Free Will 126
Tying It All Up 128
Time, Connection, and Control 131

Chapter 6 133
The Universe Inside
Are Science and Spirituality the Same Thing?....................... 133
The Universe Inside 134
Universal Moments... 135
The Greater Landscape 137
The Quantum Enigma 138
Infinite Possibilities 142
It's All Relative: e=mc2 144
Bringing It All Together 149
Religious and Spiritual Correlations 151
The Common Thread 158

Chapter 7 .... **159**
We ARE Awareness
What Do We DO With All This? 159
Aligning with Purpose 160
Balloons in the Cloudless Sky 162
Resisting What Is 163
It Is What It Is 166
Letting Go 169
The Process 171
Wearing Down the Rocks 174
The Sedona Method 176
Making Progress 179
Going Your Way 182
Beginning the Purpose Journey 183
Living in Your True Self 187
Dealing with Fear 189
Recognizing the Moment 195

Chapter 8 .... **197**
More Cloud-Clearing Practices
How Do We Reset Reality? 197
Reality Recap 197
Developing Awareness 198
Silent Meditation 200
Guided Meditation 204
Visual and Auditory Meditation 205
Mindfulness 205
Staying the Moment 208
Body Awareness 210
Self-Inquiry 212
Relaxing and Releasing 214
As Nature Intended 217

Chapter 9 219
Reality Redesigned
What Is the Broader Impact of this Worldview?.................... 219
Societal Norms 220
Ecological Drivers... 224
Health Matters.. 226
Education Reform... 231
Science vs. Philosophy 233
Pros and Cons 236

Chapter 10 238
Shall We Wrap It Up?
Our Journey 238
Addressing Unease... 242
Thoughts on Passing 244
Today, and Passing it Forward 247
Big Question Recap.. 250

About the Author 253

Endnotes... 254

Bibliography 256

Preface

It took me many years in the business world before I reached a point where I had to do something to change how I was thinking. I was fed up with the constant craving for things that never really satisfied me. I was metaphorically living in the clouds, locked into my thoughts of self and how frustrated I was because, despite the success, something was missing, and I needed to find out what it was.

You will know what I mean by this if you have reached a point where you've achieved many of your life goals yet still feel unfulfilled. The things you thought would bring you long-term happiness, be that a relationship, a house, a career, or a family, don't seem to have satisfied a more profound need within. Sure, it's great to have and to enjoy those things, but this yearning to know more appears to be growing stronger as time goes by. Or maybe you haven't experienced much of life yet, but still have this deep pull to know why you're here. You are looking around at the world you see, with its conflicts, ecological crises, and general malaise, thinking, "*Is this the world I'm going to inherit?*"

In short, if you're asking, "Is this it???"

I believe I found some answers. I'm guessing the reason you picked up or downloaded this book is to find out too. Even though

I'm not an academic and far from a guru, after learning much about the true nature of our world by digging into the scientific, psychological, and spiritual realms, I spent time integrating these learnings into daily life. It has taken several years to reach this point, and I've noticed a thread in how our lives come together. But rather than create yet another book on self-help, goal setting, or motivational techniques, I took a different approach. The viewpoints I present are a fusion of ancient and contemporary spiritual teachings, recent scientific discoveries, philosophical discussions, and psychology—and grounded in the experience of daily life.

My goal is to help you find your own answers. To walk away from this book not only with a new way of looking at your world but a new way of *living* it. To look at the blue sky and see those thunderclouds dissolve. Our lives are bursting with meaning and purpose. We are meant to be happy; as we shall see, it's our natural state.

Introduction

What's It All About?

A Google search on "the meaning of life" will return over eight billion results. Likewise, asking "What is reality?" will get you 2.6 billion and "Why do I feel dissatisfied?" over 24 million. There are so many books written, podcasts recorded, and articles posted on these questions that it seems we haven't found a satisfactory answer. Those results, however, also show an avid curiosity to understand our life purpose and what it all means. I'm guessing you're reading this book because you want a more profound understanding of life. Your own and in general. Understandably, you might be asking, "With so many opinions to choose from, what could I possibly learn here?"

I've read literally hundreds of books on these topics, and what I've found is that they are primarily written by academics or spiritual gurus who, while undeniable experts in their own fields, may not have lived a life in the cut and thrust of the real world. For most of us, life is meant to be *lived* in the world. If we're going to find out answers to these questions, they must in some way transform how we think about our lives. Otherwise, they're just more topics to contemplate as we look to our respective ceilings before sleep.

I am by no means an academic, a spiritual guru, or a philosopher. I spent many years as a marketer in various technology companies, gradually progressing up the promotional ladder. You and I are probably similar in that we live relatively everyday lives but have this gravitational pull that's hard to explain. We think we should be happy but often experience unease or discontent for no apparent reason. That feeling over several years pushed me to dig deeper into reality and how we can navigate it. Although most of my life has been spent in the business world, I've always had a keen interest in the big questions. These are the ones that tormented me most of the time,

- Who am I?
- Where did I come from?
- Why am I here?
- How should I live?
- Where am I going?

Finding the answers to these questions gives purpose to life, and, very much like a destination on a map, we need that to know that purpose so we can plot a course for our lives. Without it, we risk meandering meaninglessly, being different people to different people, feeling incomplete, and looking to people and things to relieve the emptiness.

As the gap between what I was doing with my life and the need to know my real self grew, I knew I had to do something. After reading countless books and listening to many experts, spiritual sages, scientists, philosophers, and psychologists over some twenty years, I finally saw a thread weaving through it all, indicating what was really going on and what to do with that knowledge. So I wrote it down.

Searching for Why We Feel Unfulfilled

To truly understand why we feel this way, we must consider the source of this irrational feeling of being unfulfilled. In Chapter 1, we'll look at one of the primary suspects and get familiar with that voice in our heads that's constantly talking and is seldom complimentary! Understanding the nature of this voice is critical to understanding the thoughts that fuel your emotions. Here you'll meet your Imaginary Me.

Since our experiences happen in the "real world," one of the reasons we feel unfulfilled is how we see this world. So Chapter 2 will take you on an excursion into understanding our current view of reality. Here you may find some weaknesses in your beliefs, which will uncover a deeper understanding.

Chapters 3 and 4 will be a little mind-bending but stay the course. This is where we clear away the current worldview to consider a radically alternative way to experience reality. One that is grounded in experience and intuition and provides a rational explanation of who you are and what you're here to do.

Chapter 5 continues exploring some of the fundamental aspects of our experience, including the nature of time, free will, and connection. And if you tend to be more scientific than spiritual, Chapter 6 uncovers some common threads through recent scientific discoveries and spiritual teachings that may surprise you.

The rubber hits the road in Chapter 7. Having established and validated a new way of seeing the world, this is where you'll find some practical guidance on how to apply this to your daily life. This is an experiential part of the book, inviting you to investigate what you've learned. We move on to a menu of techniques, such as meditation in Chapter 8, to help you get deeper into what you understand yourself to be and your place in the world.

You will expand your personal view of this new worldview in Chapter 9 to consider some broader implications. We'll examine the potential impact on society, education, ecology, and science in adopting a view that sees us as much more connected and similar than we believe today.

Finally, in Chapter 10, we'll pull all this together and even have a shot at answering some of those big questions that I posed earlier:

- Who am I?
- Where did I come from?
- Why am I here?
- How should I live?
- Where am I going?

I don't expect you to take what I say at face value. Rather than just believe what I say (or not!), I've included "Excursions" within each chapter. These are little breaks to sit back and experience what's being said directly rather than just reading from a page. As I mentioned above, what's being presented here is deeply experiential, so it's important to find out whether what's being said matches up to your personal experience. You're not obliged to take these excursions, but they will provide a more personal aspect of your reading. Nothing I'm saying in this book can't be arrived at by intuition if you keep an open mind.

My hope by the end of this book is that you'll have taken a profound look inside *you*, at who's *really* in there, and glimpsed a new way of viewing reality that's pregnant with meaning, with connection, with compassion. I hope this is just the start of your journey. By truly absorbing the insights you'll read here, I believe your life will change as mine did.

Okay, so let's investigate lacking fulfillment in a world crammed full of distractions and dive right into the truth of what creates these unsatisfactory feelings.

Chapter 1

Imaginary Me

Why Do We Feel Unfulfilled? What's Missing?

In those silent moments when you're not thinking about anything in particular, you might sense a deeper presence within. This presence feels quiet, content, and relaxed, but it's usually momentary. You may also find it quickly gets covered up by racing thoughts and feelings. Like you're living different lives, wearing masks that change depending on who you're talking to, what you're thinking, and how you feel.

Masking Reality

You may know what kind of person you are but are afraid to let it out. And constantly inventing personalities, changing masks, and hiding your real face—the real you—is exhausting and frustrating. Most of us live a life that is inauthentic to who we feel we really are. Often, we don't even *know* the person we are, so we use masks to create temporary replacements for a true self that is fuzzy at best. By doing this, we fit in with what we think others expect of us while feeling we're missing out on something important.

Imaginary Me

I used to imagine lying on my deathbed, looking up at off-white hospital ceiling tiles with the smell of disinfectant in my nose, thinking: *"Was that it then...?"* That feeling used to terrify me. To have spent eighty or so years on this planet without at least attempting to understand who I really was. To not respond to that pull to know more about the world and to get a glimpse at my reason for being here before my time runs out. It simply didn't make sense to me that, for most of us, we work hard to acquire things, only to have them disappear, along with our bodies, memories, and experiences, instantly—at any instant. That was just unacceptable. I was halfway through my life and realized I had to find some stuff out or sit back and wait for those ceiling tiles. I'm sure you've had similar experiences. When it finally dawns on you that *this is my life*. Nothing is more important than ensuring you live it well.

It is also true that many of us relate living well with achievement and financial success and the belief that goes with it: *"If I work hard now, then in the future I will have that huge house on the coast, that orange Lamborghini, a couple Rolexes, and a summer home. Then I'll be happy."* But even if we achieve that success, does it make a well-lived life? How many affluent people become addicted to drugs, some even dying?

I've talked to many successful people, and almost all of them say that, although they have an initial "high" when they get what they desire, they still feel "not good enough," regardless of how much they accumulate. They either become more frustrated that the need isn't being filled, or they look for the next hit. Why settle

Cloudless Reality

for $100 million when you could have $200? Then I'll be okay. Likewise, we experience people, maybe you know some, that have little in the way of material things in comparison to most of us yet are the happiest people we know. Why is that? Could it be that when we can't be distracted by the acquisition and subsequent addiction to material things, we settle into our true selves for happiness?

Perhaps you feel that life is like a balance between what you are doing versus what you would rather do. Where you are living a life, but it seems to have little meaning, and that makes us feel unhappy. If you ask yourself frequently, *"What is the point of my doing this?"* you're not aligned with what you're here to do. You may not have a clear alternative to what you would rather do instead, but you know it's not what you're doing right now. Many of us have lived in that balance for many years. I did. Job after job, role after role, home after home, car after car, in a constant battle between being an external *display* and an internal *person*. We're often in complete ignorance of this balance while always being led by the constant narration in our heads.

Imaginary Me

You hear the voice in there, right? The one that's continually talking. Sometimes to you, sometimes to itself, and almost always with an opinion. It usually comes to us as a series of images and narrations around a story, and they are almost always negative, critical, or wanting things to be different. We all have that voice. I call it the "Imaginary Me" because, as you'll see, it is totally unreal. It's an illusion, and while illusions are real in themselves (just think about a magic trick, you *do* experience an illusion), what you *believe* to be real in the illusion, is not. Rather like a permanent and noisy roommate inside your head, this illusory self is always seeking or avoiding something. It can never be completely satisfied for long, as that wanting is how it exists. It is also very difficult to quieten this voice. If you try to push it away, it seems to feed on that effort and comes back stronger. Surprisingly, we seldom pay attention to what that voice is saying. It's usually just some background noise. That background noise, however, can influence our thoughts, emotions, and actions, often without our knowing. Pause for a moment and listen to this voice right now. This is the first of our little trips inward!

> Take a moment to relax and close your eyes. Take a few deep breaths as you transition from an external to an internal focus. Don't think about anything specifically. Rather let your thoughts and feelings come up naturally. Just watch those thoughts. You may start to get invested in them, and that's fine. Just let this thought show play for a minute or two, then come back to the book.

If you're anything like me, when I first started paying attention to my thoughts, it felt totally chaotic and out of control. Several observations came to mind for me.

Firstly, *"Wow, it really is crazy in there!"* Random thoughts and feelings constantly coming and going, some extremely loud and persuasive. Most of them I'm not consciously choosing to experience; they just come up unannounced. *Do I have any control over what I think most of the time?* Imagine speaking out loud the things you hear "inside"? If you were walking down the street and giving an external voice to that internal one, you'd soon be sitting in a home for the permanently bewildered! You may also note that it isn't always just speaking to you but to itself, too, as if it is multiple entities.

I also found a pattern to what I was thinking and feeling. Almost everything that came into my awareness was focused on either something that happened in the past or something that might happen in the future. I could also clearly see that there was always a need for things to be different. Whether about the current situation or a thought, nothing was good enough. Either it was unwanted and needed to change, or it was good and needed to stay. The content of the dialog was often pointless too. Rather like a child thrashing around in a tantrum, the things being said or felt were random and, at times, felt desperate. It was fascinating and intimidating at the same time. It really wasn't something I wanted to spend a lot of time looking at. Which is why most of us don't.

When you do choose to look at what's going on in there, it might rather feel like tuning in to a radio station. The "noise" doesn't appear just when we choose to pay attention; it's constantly broadcasting with a variable volume dial we often can't control.

Imaginary Me

When that volume dial is turned up past a certain point, the feeling registers and stays with us. There's often no rationale for why the dial is turned up; it is one of life's challenges. This is *your* radio; you have control of it. You've just ceded that control to someone else. Like this:

"*Blah, blah, blah, oh, there's a car like mine, blah, blah, blah, I should call Sally, blah, blah, blah, you look fat today, blah, blah, blah . . .*"

Wait . . . the dial just got turned way up!

"*. . . Hang on, what was that? I look fat. Actually, I do feel fat. I also feel sad now. I eat too much; I have no willpower. . .*"

There you go. Drawn into the gravitational pull of a random, invented story in a maelstrom of ramblings. That comment may have been triggered by something you've just experienced or maybe by nothing. Just an out-of-the-blue comment from a voice somewhere "back there" that didn't seem to come from you. Sound familiar?

It's Not Real

These stories, in the form of thoughts, images, and feelings, are unreal. They are just experiences that pass through your field of awareness in the same way that "*Oh, there's a car like mine*" or "*I should call Sally?*" pass you by. The difference is you pay more attention to certain stories that have their volume jacked up. That familiar car passes by also in a random way, not of your choice, but is quickly a thing of the past. Unless you have a thing about similar

Cloudless Reality

cars to yours, that experience passes without a second thought. However, *"you look fat today"* doesn't pass you by. It latches onto something inside you. Both the car and the comment are the same thing. They are merely images that happen to be passing by in the world. Neither means anything. There are reasons why one story stays and another leaves, and we'll get into that later, but trust me when I say that of the thoughts and feelings you experience, 97 percent are "baseless and result from an unfounded pessimistic perception."[1]

Although it may seem counterintuitive, part of our purpose in life is to live happily with this opinionated roommate. This internal voice is as integral to us as our heart, lungs, and big toes. Living happily with it, however, doesn't mean being *directed by it,* and the reason why almost all of us feel so incomplete is because we've allowed this voice to direct us. We've had no option because we created it and can't see it unless we make ourselves look.

Of thoughts you experience, 97 percent are baseless and result from an unfounded pessimistic perception.

This illusion can be very powerful. The more you buy into the stories it tells you, the more power you give it. With that power comes its ability to influence and ultimately dictate your life. Rather like a frog slowly boiling in a pan of hot water, it creeps up over the years, unnoticed, until eventually, you *are* it.

Since this is happening to everyone, our generally accepted view of the world has been defined by this collective illusion, and so, as we shall see, our current worldview is itself an illusion. A life dictated to by this false self is not your true life, not the life you were meant to live, and trust me, you were meant to live a happy and peaceful life, not "fat and sad!"

This divide between your real self and this internal voice in control is one of the core reasons for feelings of incompleteness and unhappiness. That isn't surprising, given the negatively charged nature of the illusion in control. If you had a real person next to you, constantly whispering in your ear that *"you're not good enough," "you're a fake," "you can't do it,"* you would either stop listening or believe it and live in a constant state of discomfort. Unfortunately, most of us do the latter. The good news is you do have that choice.

From Prunes to iPads

When my daughter was young, before four years old, maybe, I would look at how she reacted to and interacted with the world. She was either happy or not happy, and that was really it. There were no other obvious emotions. When she was eating food that she loved (pureed prunes, believe it or not), she had a big smile. When she was tired or cranky, the tears came, accompanied by surprisingly high-decibel cries. While the emotions were often pronounced, it was amazing to me how they could change in an instant. That there seemed no remnant of the emotion once it had passed. I also loved how she was often in a state of fascination, curiosity, and wonder at even the simplest of things. A teddy, a spoon, a flower, a face, you name it, she looked to be investigating it, and usually with a big smile (unless she was cranky!).

Cloudless Reality

I think anyone with kids can associate with this somehow, but we see the same thing with animals. Discipline a dog, and it will react with guilt-ridden eyes looking up at you with its tail down between its legs, but all you need do is say, "Good boy" or "Good girl" with a smile, and all is forgotten. Literally forgotten. That is now in the past. The dog doesn't dwell on why it was in trouble in the first place. What would the point of that be? The dog just moves on. Admittedly this is harder with cats. They never feel guilty about anything!

We were all innocently curious at that young age, regardless of who, where, and when we came into this world. You may not remember it now as an adult. Have you ever made eye contact with a baby? I mean *real* eye contact. I did once, on a New York City subway train. That little person stared at me with what seemed to be complete wonder. Almost as if they had never seen a human face before. Those small, brown-eyes (yes I remember the eye color!) kept my gaze for what seemed like minutes. It triggered a strong emotional response in me that I've never forgotten. It felt weird to say it at the time, but it really felt as if I was looking at me, looking at me. It just went deeper and deeper until I was probably looking weird on the train, so stopped the staring!

You can probably remember times when, as an adult, you experienced a feeling of awe when everything around just seemed to fall away. Looking at the stars on a clear night, falling in love for the first time, seeing a humpback whale calf up close from a kayak in Maui (one of my personal bests!). I want you to remember that feeling because that is who you are all the time. It is who we all are. We've just forgotten.

When my daughter was around five or six, things started to change. I would still see the same wonder and excitement, but more often, it was in response to maybe receiving a toy or candy or when she got what she wanted (did someone say iPad?). Disappointment and sadness still came when she was tired, but they also cropped up when she didn't get what she expected (did someone say iPad??). Or when things were taken away from her, including objects (candy) and experiences (can't go to the zoo today).

By the time she was seven, my daughter had clearly developed a liking for certain things and a dislike for others. These preferences began to form her personality, so I knew which experiences would trigger a strong emotional reaction, positive and negative. Positive emotions stayed around relatively briefly, compared to negative emotions—which could stay for hours, even days. A far cry from the earlier years when any emotion was gone and forgotten within a few seconds. I now know this was the start of her subconsciously retaining strong emotional responses as a means of self-protection from similar experiences in the future.

Fast forward to today, and this is how personality is formed. There's really nothing wrong with that. How else should it develop, if not from personal experiences and memories? These make us unique and give meaning to our lives. But it isn't our actual experiences that are problematic. As you'll see later, whether good or bad, slight or traumatic, having experiences is why we're here in the first place. If we didn't have them, life would be pointless, meaningless, and perhaps a little boring. It's rather our irrational *attachment* to certain experiences that gets us into trouble.

Accumulating more and more irrational attachments to experiences causes us to lose our sense of raw wonder, replacing it with opinions on just about everything. This is the birth of the Imaginary Me. We don't do this intentionally. This illusory self is an accumulation of all the highly charged emotional experiences we've stored inside ourselves. As we'll see, there is a reason why we store them, and seeing the truth of this is one way to set yourself free of them.

> *It is our irrational attachment to certain experiences that gets us into trouble.*

Experiences are meant to simply come and go across our field of perception. We are meant to learn from them, to remember some of them, to use them for productive and positive things, but their nature is temporary. An experience may generate thoughts and emotions, but these, too, are meant to be temporary. Just there to be experienced in the moment. After they have passed, they no longer exist in reality. When we hold onto any of them emotionally, we hold onto a phantom.

Hence the persona created from the accumulation of these held emotions is itself illusionary. It's literally made from charged past experiences that no longer exist. They are trapped inside and build up to form an unstable and fragmented version of our "self." This self believes itself to be incomplete. Built on illusory preferences and an ideal of how the world should be, it is by its very nature

Imaginary Me

paranoid, defensive, and fearful.

It's quite surprising to learn, then, that almost all of us buy into the stories from this illusory self to the point that we believe that is who we really are. Since this persona isn't real, it's never whole, and it feels it deeply. This is the source of our feelings of incompleteness. Your real, authentic self is completely whole and always has been. If you're not feeling complete, then it's likely that some aspects of this illusory mind are running your life. Don't feel bad. There are about seven billion people in the same situation (although most either don't know it or won't admit it).

The illusory self can never replace any part of the real you. It just obscures it from view, like a cloud obscuring the sky. You are always present as that sky, trying to shine through a false self. The Imaginary Me and your true self are aspects of you, but one is just an illusion. As we shall see, you can see through this illusion and reveal more of that sky.

The real you is much closer to a four-year-old living in wonder than the illusory personality you are today. Think about yourself today. Right now, actually.

Sit back, relax, close your eyes, and ask yourself: "Am I in there?"

Is there a "someone" who is reading or listening to this book right now? If someone asked you, "Who are you?" What would you say? "I'm a middle-aged woman with a good job and a nice house living in France."

Okay, sounds lovely. So that's who you think you are. If you weren't living in France, you wouldn't be that person then, right? Or if you had a different job, you'd be a different person? Obviously, the "you" in there isn't defined by external circumstances.

How about internal circumstances, such as thoughts and feelings. "I'm depressed'. You weren't always depressed? So, who were you before you were depressed? Maybe you define yourself by your body, "I'm an overweight sixty-five-year-old male with failing eyesight." Have you always been that way? You certainly haven't always been in your sixties.

Okay, come back and let's chat!

As you know from your experience, objects, thoughts, and feelings drift across your perception continuously. You observe thousands of objects daily, from traffic lights to chairs. You just have to close your eyes to experience the myriad thoughts that come and go. Same with emotions. You may have experienced intense nervousness before standing to speak to a crowd for example, but was that same feeling there when you stepped down? When you think about it, everything we experience is in a state of constant change. Even your physical body is in constant flux. About 330 billion human cells are replaced daily, equivalent to about 1 percent of all our cells.[2] In eighty to a hundred days, thirty trillion will have been replenished—the equivalent of a new you. So just like your thoughts and emotions, your physical body is also transient.

Although all the "things" we define as being ourselves (our bodies, thoughts, and emotions) constantly change, we seem to maintain an internal state of continuity throughout our lives. We feel a sense of "me" that is the same regardless of where and when we are. You can take a moment to sense it right now. Undoubtedly there is a "me" reading or listening to this book. That same "me" was there when you were two years old. Still there when you were a teenager and will be there when you die. It knows how you felt when you were hungry at six months old. It knows how devastated you were when you were dumped as a teenager.

Try to get a sense of this continuity of "me" for a minute or so.

Think back to a memorable time in the more distant past. Perhaps from your school days or an early birthday party. Try to put yourself in your own body back then and relive the experience, even for just a few seconds. Now fast forward a few years. It doesn't matter how far. Do the same in-body exercise again. Fast forward to a recent event, perhaps a few weeks ago, and repeat. It's worth spending a few minutes trying to experience this. Now come back.

You likely experienced a similar sense of "me" in all those memories. Even taking a pause to experience the "me" reading this book will possibly show the same sense of self is present. You will have had very different thoughts, emotions, opinions, and environments, and even your body will have been quite different through each scenario. However, this "me" sense was consistent. What that "me" is, we'll get into later but suffice it to say there is a continual presence within us, and it's the key to our freedom.

It's what we commonly refer to as "I."

We're just touching on this now, but as you progress through the book, you'll discover the most important thing you will ever know regarding your life. I know that sounds dramatic, but it is truthful to say that this is the core of who we are based purely on experience. It has also been the root of all religious and spiritual teachings through millennia. If there is an "I" that never changes, but has always been aware of the transient objects, thoughts, feelings, and experiences throughout your life, then this "I" must be who you really are.

Let me spell this out a little more directly.

> You are not your body,
> You are not your thoughts,
> You are not your emotions.
> The real you is what is aware of them.

The "I" never changes. It never "is" anything. It is just aware *of* everything. What exactly is it aware of? Experiences. Although we'll investigate the nature of this "I" in detail in the coming chapters, I mention it here for an important reason. The very fact that we can investigate this consistent sense of "me" is because it is being observed. If it is being observed, it cannot be what is being observed! It's something else. If you consider the exercise above, in all those times past you recalled, how did you know that there was a consistent "me" throughout? Let's focus a little more on the cause of our discomfort and see how it

If there is an "I" that never changes, but has always been aware of the transient objects, thoughts, feelings, and experiences throughout your life, then this "I" must be who you really are.

came to be. We'll get to know "you" a little more later.

Building an Imaginary Me

Any experience can be categorized as either an "object" (a table, a car, a flower, your body), "emotion" (sadness, happiness, anger, fear), or "thought" (just about anything, but usually negative and fear-based thoughts). These three entities are constantly interacting to create our world. They are vitally important for us to function and thrive in life, and as such, they can be wonderful experiences. If we couldn't experience objects, we'd have no reference point to live our lives and we couldn't effectively interact with others. Without thoughts, we'd never have invented the wheel, discovered fire, or built Amazon! If we didn't feel our emotions, we'd be zombies without empathy or purpose. It's doubtful humans could have evolved without the ability to perceive these things, so they are an inherent part of our evolution.

As we've said, however, through a need to protect ourselves from harm (even imagined harm), we misuse these objects of experience to create a fragmented alternative version of ourselves, very much like a bodyguard preventing you from getting to see your true self.

Here's how our illusory self is created. As we grow past that magical four-year-old stage of raw perception, we begin to process information from our experiences more contextually. We combine our direct experiences of objects, thoughts, and feelings with information we're given about them. This information comes from myriad sources, but most commonly parents, friends, school, TV, the internet, books, and life experiences. It doesn't matter whether this information is right or wrong. At that young age, we don't know any difference; we just believe what we're told.

Let's look at this process through a simple scenario. You are four years old in your parent's garden one fine summer day, and you see a rose growing nearby. You've never seen one before. Looking closely, you see this is as possibly the most amazing thing you've ever seen. The bright red petals, the feel of the stem, the beautiful aroma. Since you haven't been told what a rose is yet, you have no thoughts about the rose, no judgment. Just the raw experience of the flower itself.

Suddenly, you prick your thumb on one of the thorns. That wasn't expected. It causes surprise, physical pain and threatens your well-being. You see drops of blood on your finger. Hysterical, you run to tell your parents what happened. Your parents tell you that roses can be very dangerous due to their thorns and that the prick on your finger must be cleaned immediately otherwise it could get infected and hurt even more and for longer. The rose experience triggers a strong emotional reaction. Your self-protection mechanism kicks in and grabs that emotion, storing it as a reminder of the experience.

Here's the unfortunate thing: you may now fear, maybe even hate, roses—and may do so for the rest of your life. Not just roses, maybe any flower with thorns. Maybe even flowers—period. What started as a magical, wonderful experience with nature turned into a long-term fear in about ten seconds. The fear arising from that experience creates another piece of the Imaginary Me. There was nothing you could have done to prevent that; it was part of nature doing its thing. What is unnatural, however, is that this kid may never relish seeing a rose again due to the fictional story of the deadly nature of roses written decades ago.

If you imagine the rose scenario applied to multiple everyday experiences—from something trivial like a pair of red socks turning everything in the wash a light pink hue (never buys red clothes again) to being dumped for the first time by a girl with blonde hair (never dates blondes again)—all our preferences, come down to our past experiences. Not the experience itself (there's nothing wrong with red socks), but the experience combined with information that, in most cases, was someone else's preference (dad saying that roses can kill). We are often unaware of that extra information. We just feel a highly charged reaction and respond accordingly. This is why some people can see a spider and be fine. Others will react with abject terror. Someone either had a negative experience with a spider (were bitten maybe) or, more likely, acquired some additional information that created a fear of spiders. Perhaps they watched a TV show on tarantulas when they were young that stayed with them, or an older sibling told a scary story about spiders when they were a toddler.

The Emotion Store

When we experience events with a high emotional charge (either positive or negative), we tend to automatically store or trap those emotions. We do this for self-protection, so we can avoid similar negative emotions in the future (like the body's immune system) or strive to recreate a positive one. The problem is that storing the emotion causes it to "bloat" or be exaggerated into unwanted feelings such as fear (of either having a repeat negative emotion or not getting a repeat positive one). These emotions can stay trapped within us for our entire lives. When we let these emotions go, we clean up our inner state.

We experience "things" every second of our lives—grass, the sun and moon across the sky, cars on the freeway, the feeling of the floor beneath our feet. None of those experiences seem to bother us. They are things we experience all the time that pass through our observation. Experiences that have a high emotional charge to them (roses, socks, spiders, and blondes) are the ones that tend to stick around. They are almost always accompanied by our vocal roommate, that ties the unwanted emotion to a (mostly negative) story:

"Uh oh, we're walking into a garden. I'll bet there'll be roses. Can't stand that smell. Let's leave."

"She's a nice girl, and I know she likes you, but she's blonde. Not going to work, buddy. Talk to her brunette girlfriend instead."

"I don't do the laundry in our family. Don't know why. I just don't like doing it. I'll do anything else."

Multiply this a million-fold, and you build what begins to feel like an individual personality. A version of you based purely on all these misconceived preferences and stories. Since this "version" of you is built from an early age, you haven't the faculties at that point to see that there is a genuine you beneath the façade. Hence you are left with no choice but to see this illusory self as the real you. That is how we grow up.

Cloudless Reality

Like a fish in water, most of us are so immersed in these preferences that we don't even know we are being run by them. They dictate almost everything we do, defining our relationships and careers, even crafting an imaginary life purpose because of a positive or negative experience: "You're really good at numbers, so your purpose must be to be the best accountant in the world" or "I can't budget, I'm no mathematician." Most of us die without knowing that the "persona" we've been living as our lives has not been our true selves but a self-created illusion. The only inclination we may have that that is the case will be the "Is that it?" question getting louder and louder as the days go by and the real you tries to shine through.

The illusion is simply driven by either wanting or not-wanting things to be a certain way. These two drivers are most often felt as fear, worry, anxiety, greed, a feeling of being "not enough," you know those feelings. It finds solace in the mistaken belief that it must protect you by having control over you, therefore defining you as an individual and separate thing in the world, having only yourself to protect. Our predominant material worldview is one in which everyone is separate, where resources are limited, and we live a short time, so we must accumulate as much "stuff" as possible before we die. This worldview serves to normalize the protective actions of the illusory mind. Hence it is undetectable to most of us. More on this vicious cycle later.

> *The accumulation of material things, experiences, hostilities, and greed are all rooted in the need for the Imaginary Me to exist and to protect itself, and it is based on fiction.*

Imaginary Me

It's easy to see how this illusion is the root of all negative thoughts and emotions, including the need to be better, be right, be stronger, be richer, be more attractive. The accumulation of material things, experiences, hostilities, and greed are all rooted in the need for the Imaginary Me to exist and to protect itself, and it is based on fiction.

It may be tempting to consider all your thoughts and feelings, however transient, to be an integral part of who you are. That they are there to help guide you in the right direction. It is true that when thoughts and feelings are aligned with your true purpose, they can help you move forward as supporting mechanisms, and when this happens, you will intuitively know. Most of the time, however, the stories weaved by the mind are quite random, with no purpose other than to tell self-critical stories of the past and, more often, to create a fabricated future that seldom comes to fruition.

> Think back to experiences where you were certain that the outcome of a given situation would be bad for you. Maybe you thought you would lose your job, run out of money, or get divorced. There may be a potential scenario you're dreading right now. Be honest—how many of those "worse-case" scenarios actually happened? Or if they did happen, were they as awful as you assumed they were going to be?

Cloudless Reality

When I think about this, it's clear that almost every future scenario my mind tells me could happen never has. Or if it has, it's nowhere near as dreadful as I assumed it would be. Similarly, with past experiences, what I often recall is far more severe than the experiences other people involved had in that same event. In short, the stories our imaginary self tells us are mostly fabrications and exaggerations. In that respect, it is altogether healthier to consider them mostly a work of fiction—an illusion that you can choose to dissolve. But how?

Dissolving the Illusion

The conundrum we humans find ourselves in then is this. Our true nature, as we shall see, is wholeness. No lack. No discontent. In fact, it is the very definition of happiness. Perhaps ironically, the illusory self is defined by the exact opposite. Fragmentation, constant lacking, and a pervasive feeling of discontent. Since we intuitively know our true nature, and the illusion seems to be the opposite of that, we already have what we need to deal with the illusion. We just need the will to see it and do something about it.

Simple though it may seem, as with anything that seeks our attention, if you ignore the stories you're being fed and don't get pulled into its drama, your voice will soon tire of bothering you and stop. It really is as simple as that. In fact, there isn't anything to attain or achieve in minimizing the impact of the illusion. Returning to "you" is more like losing weight than striving for some enlightened state. People have been practicing "disbelieving the voice" for thousands of years. We just need to get back to that four-year-old and love pureed prunes again!

So, let's look to "thin-out" the Imaginary Me. Reduce the chasm between who you have always believed you are and who you really are. As that gap reduces, so do your feelings of incompleteness. But before we embark on an understanding of how to deal with the illusory self, it's important to set the context of the view of reality in which we all operate. The reason why this illusion has been able to garner so much control over us is symptomatic of the way we have been taught to see the world; the two are totally intertwined. So to get to the source of our dissatisfaction and examine those big questions rationally, we must first understand how most of us see the world today and then open the door to a radical new way of looking at reality.

Chapter 2

Getting Perspective

What Is Your Current View of Reality?

The world around us is fundamentally different from the world as it really is. So to get to the heart of why you're here and why you probably feel, as so many of us do, as though there should be more to life, let's explore the "here and now" and how it relates to life's purpose. Since the world is only what you can experience of it, then objects, thoughts, emotions, even the illusory mind, and the conscious observer all exist in what we call the "real world."

Defining the Real World

So, what exactly is the real world? Before we get to that, let's first look at the worldview created through the illusory self. Several aspects of our current worldview are aligned with the needs and desires of this self that don't stand the test of rational inspection. We'll dive deeper into the drivers of this part of our mind and how those drivers form our worldview today.

We'll also look experientially at basic concepts, such as objects we perceive, and again put that to a rational test. We will be

Getting Perspective

questioning the mainstream view of what physical things really are and how closely they are related to your thoughts and feelings.

In the previous chapter, we discussed how the accumulation of experiences you either didn't want to happen or crave happening again creates an illusory personality, the Imaginary Me, that, for all intents and purposes, is running your life. Like a computer program, it just runs its course day by day, year by year. It's estimated that around half of our daily activities[3] consist of "unconscious" repetitious habits (brushing your teeth, driving to work, checking the phone, etc.). While most of these practical habits are not unhealthy, we all know myriad unwelcome thoughts plague us routinely and randomly.

"Still putting on weight, I see, no self-control. You'll never find anyone looking like that."

"More gray hairs? You're running out of time, pal. You need to get that promotion before it's too late."

Let's be honest; it's difficult to ignore the commentary. We are so intimate with the voice that the experience isn't that of a separate entity telling stories to you. It is YOU telling the stories to yourself. Why wouldn't you believe them? We even maintain this belief when we hear more than one voice talking to another while "we" listen in.

Voice 1: "Should I wear the blue skirt or the grey skirt?"

Voice 2: "The blue skirt makes you look too formal; you should wear the grey one."

"Voice 3: "But the grey one is too tight, which would be uncomfortable, and you'll be annoyed by it all day."

Cloudless Reality

Voice 1: "Geez, why can't you just make a decision for once!!?"

Sound familiar? We unconsciously believe there is a clear dialog between multiple "voices," yet this is contrary to our real world. That's how embedded we are with this illusion. Again, consider how you can know these voices are there. Who is it that hears them? The paradox is that we think we *are* the voices, yet we also know that we're observing those very voices.

Let's take an excursion to listen to the types of thoughts we experience.

Close your eyes and watch what's happening in your mind. Listen for a voice, feeling, or thought without thinking about anything. It may take a few seconds, or you may be inundated with thoughts and feelings; either way is good. Now open your eyes and consider this question. Did you believe you had any control over the thoughts and feelings that came up? Be honest, this is important.

It's estimated that some 95 percent of our daily thoughts are not ones we have consciously decided to think about.[4] That's a huge proportion! So, who does have control? Where do the thoughts come from, and why? Most of those random thoughts, especially the ones that have their root in either wanting something or pushing something away, are your illusory mind at work. It doesn't need your conscious agency to bring up thoughts. It's quite content creating its own.

Exactly *where* these thoughts come from is one of the most enigmatic questions you can ask, and we will get to that question later in the book. *Why* they come up and what they represent depends on the individual. The Imaginary Me is constructed from many suppressed personal experiences, and no two people has the same set of experiences. What we do know is that these thoughts are being created to protect you. We've mentioned this before, but let's dig deeper now.

> *The Imaginary Me is constructed from many suppressed personal experiences, and no two people can have the same set of experiences.*

Self-Protection Mode

This illusory persona was originally born out of a need to protect you from physical harm. Harking back to a time when the only things we needed protection from were those that threatened our physical existence, it's proved extremely astute at serving our needs. However, for the most part, humanity has evolved past the point where we need protection from physical threats, so the illusory self turns to protect us from psychological threats instead. Rather than tell us stories about how we need to find food and shelter lest we starve or freeze, it now uses the same powerful influence on us to tell stories about how we're not good enough, or too fat, too thin, that the world is out to get us.

Extending beyond protection from threats as they come, the

illusory self even creates its own threats to perpetuate its existence. Most of these random imagined threats surface in those 95 percent of thoughts we don't control. It's as though there's another "person" inside us with their own thoughts and feelings that impinge on our own and influence us. Although the intent is protection, you don't need to be protected from imaginary psychological threats as you do physical harm. These threats have no basis in what's real and cannot affect your emotional state unless you give them that power. Withdrawing power from them, as we shall see, is a big part of what it takes to become free of negative feelings.

What about the remaining 5 percent of intentional thoughts? These thoughts are functional and do (and should) have the power to change your state. Thoughts such as, *"I have to switch the gas off on the stove when I'm done,"* keep us safe. These thoughts are a correct use of the personal mind, as are creativity, problem-solving, caring for others, etc. Humanity used this 5 percent to discover the atom, put people on the moon, write countless beautiful symphonies, and build societies. These are examples of the correct use of the personal mind and is why we have such a mind in the first place. When aligned with our real selves, the human mind is a magnificent tool. As far as we know, nothing like it exists in the universe. However, we pay a price for our brilliance.

The Gift of Introspection

As far as we know, we (and maybe apes, dolphins, and possibly other species, since research is actively ongoing here,[5] are the only animals capable of introspection—that is, "we know that we know." When we are hungry, we know we are hungry. We can step back, observe ourselves and decide we must get food. When a dog is hungry, however, it IS hunger. Dogs and most other species lack the capacity to step back and decide they are hungry. They *become* the emotion of hunger and so seek food.

Introspection is a unique human capability, and as we shall see, it is key to finding meaning in life. When you can step back and analyze yourself and your actions, then you can improve, evolve, and thrive; and that's just what we did. Effectively a form of "conscious evolution," we use our introspection to iteratively improve ourselves and our world. Introspection is why humans are head and shoulders the most evolved species on the planet. We possess a unique form of consciousness that, as we will see, has taken a disproportionately long evolutionary period to surface.

This tremendous ability, however, can also be used to reflect on unwanted emotions and to make a conscious or unconscious decision to push them away from our cognition (what Freud would call "suppression" or "repression," respectively). It is this meta-cognitive act of recognizing and pushing away unwanted experiences (either real or imagined) throughout our lives that trap our emotions and help construct the Imaginary Me.

With introspection, we have at once the ability to look inward to improve and look inward to suppress. We cannot separate these actions. They are part of the same "you," and as we'll see, this is necessary for our growth. When the illusory self is in control, which it is most of the time, it uses this ability to create irrational criticism. For example, rather than *"It's okay to learn from your mistakes,"* we hear, *"You shouldn't have made that mistake. You're a failure again!"* To make both statements, you first must be able to see the mistake. This is introspection. Can you guess which statement is real versus imaginary?

It's easy to tell the difference between irrational criticism and necessary, healthy introspection—the quality of your feelings at the time.

The key to maximizing the potential of introspection, without the resulting unreasonable criticism that comes along with it, is to not get involved in that unreasonable criticism in the first place. Just take the illusion for what it is. Simply an illusion that cannot affect you unless you choose to believe it. It's easy to tell the difference between irrational criticism and necessary, healthy introspection—the quality of your feelings at the time. Whenever you look inward and form a constructive conclusion, with no negative self-talk, that's a correct use of introspection that will move you in a forward direction. Everything else is imaginary.

Our introspective abilities, when driven by the illusory mind, can quickly convert everyday thoughts and feelings into monsters that generate fear and anxiety. The Imaginary Me is an expert at exaggerating the innocent into the "worse-case scenario." It needs to quickly accelerate mundane experiences into the worse case to fully reinforce its existence. Look back on your own life. Can you imagine instances where a simple thought quickly snowballed into a potential disaster? If so, did that disaster materialize? Look at the examples below which illustrate this:

Example 1
Thought
"I should get a new car. This one is getting old."
Escalation
"If you don't get the car, you'll feel miserable and a failure. Sarah just bought a brand new one."
Feeling
Sadness. Greed. Desperation. Comparisons.

Example 2
Thought
"I didn't like the tone of that email from my boss."
Escalation
"You're gonna lose your job. If you lose the job, you'll be homeless within days."
Feeling
Fear. Anticipation. Guilt.

Example 3
Thought
"I wonder why the TV won't switch on."
Escalation
"Probably broken, and it was expensive too. We'll have to replace it. Why do these things happen to me?"
Feeling
Anger. Guilt. Wounded.

Take a moment to pause and experience and reflect on any similar worse-case imaginings in your life right now. It doesn't matter how big or small they are. You could be clinging to a relationship or the consequences of forgetting to take out the trash. See if what I'm saying resonates with you. Even better if you can hear or sense the escalating voice when you pull up a thought.

Experiencing this for yourself, rather than taking my word, will allow you to step into observer mode, and it is this state that will, with practice, help you break through the clouds of the illusionary mind.

Much Ado Over a Chip

I once had a chip in a wooden floorboard in my apartment. It was tiny and would be missed by most people. Whenever I walked by that chip, I would think, *"Must fix that before someone gets a splinter."* Positive and useful introspection at that point would make a note to fix that chip. That's it.

Immediately, however, the voice would take over, releasing the following torrent: *"You're never going to fix that. You're a procrastinator. You're probably procrastinating about other things, too, like that big project at work. Carry on doing that, and you'll lose the job, then you won't have to worry about the chip anymore; you'll be on the sidewalk asking for change!"*

All that would come up in about a second every time I walked by a half-inch chip in a piece of wood. Ironically, the feelings induced by that commentary distracted me from fixing the chip every time. The voice's message was received loud and clear in my uncontrolled thoughts and resulted in the very procrastination it predicted!

Although most of the time, I tried to ignore the voice, the experience always left me with a residual feeling of inadequacy. Even after I'd forgotten about the chip, and possibly for hours afterward, I would often experience memories of past times when I'd been disappointed in myself, along with the accompanying feelings. How can a chipped floorboard do that? The rational part of the mind notices the chip, sees the potential consequence, and decides to act. The illusory mind notices this and chimes in, lest it gets relegated further down the food chain. It tells an exaggerated story that's barely connected to the event but stirs up charged emotions, nevertheless. See how it's not the experience itself but the *voice* that takes the experience and expands it beyond the rational? And if you buy into this sort of irrational fiction, you feel bad and often have no idea why. When this happens many times a day (as it often does), the resulting negative feelings become a constant background noise. This is why, for many of the "urgh" feelings we tend to have, we can't identify why they exist. They surface from an amalgamation of such experiences over time.

It's not hard to see the lengths your internal voice will go to provide what it believes is self-protection is mostly illusionary.

Cloudless Reality

Ultimately the response back from the voice to any thoughts, be they proactively created or not, is also unreal. If you can interject at the point that the voice chimes in and pull your attention away from it (not fight it or suppress it), you're on the path to freedom. You just need to be aware of the escalation potential of the voice. It's been doing this since you were four and has gotten very astute at it!

Ultimately the response back from the voice to any thoughts, be they proactively created or not, is also unreal

When I could finally pause at the point where the voice barged in as I passed by my chip, recognizing it for what it was and letting it go (as we'll talk about in Chapter 7), it was fixed in the next half hour. Instantly, all those important comments about procrastination just melted away as if they never existed. No residual regret and, most importantly, no splinters!

It's All About Me

At the start of the book, I described that everything we can ever possibly know is only available to us through our subjective experience. Since our thoughts and emotions are created through our interactions with the world, and many of these thoughts and emotions create a sense of discontentment and emptiness, let's delve a little further into how we see this world. Specifically, let's focus on how we think about things we accumulate, our experiences, and how personal they can often be to us.

Let's start by looking at objects that we desire. When most people see an object, let's say a car, they assume (with good reason on the

Getting Perspective

face of it) that the car has been built by engineers and mechanics to move people around. Some could see the car as a simple means of transportation. Others may see it as a representation of something more than that. Perhaps as a status symbol, helping to reinforce a desired image of themselves. We also know that over time the car will get older, will wear out, and degrade. Eventually, the car will cease to be useable and disappear from most people's perception as a car (perhaps in pieces at a scrapyard).

This example offers two important observations. Firstly, the same physical object can have different meanings to different people, and secondly, physical objects have a finite existence in time. You can apply this to any object "out there," be it a car, a house, an elephant, or another human. This subjectivity of object experience and the temporal limitation of objects are seen from the viewpoint of the illusory mind as the following:

- Objects are totally separate from me, and my opinion is the only correct one.
- Objects are finite in time, including us, so we must accumulate as many of them as possible before it's too late.

Let's break these two observations down.

Perceiving Objects as Separate from Me

As we've discussed, how we experience the world is always filtered by our accumulated experiences. Since everyone's life experience is unique, no two people will experience the same object similarly. Like looking at the world through tinted glasses, there

Cloudless Reality

is an objective world out there, but how we perceive it will differ depending on the extent to which our glasses are tinted.

We may see an object as similar (a car is a car), but that object is as personal as our fingerprint. In its "protection mode," the illusory self seeks to create harmony between the perceived outside world and our internal preferences. It does this by trying to change the outside world since the internal world is believed to be the only real one. It will do this forcefully at times. Remember, the basis of the illusory mind is physical self-preservation. It needed to be compelling to keep us from bodily harm. This is why we defend an internally created point of view vehemently and often irrationally.

> *In its "protection mode," the illusory self seeks to create harmony between the perceived outside world and our internal preferences.*

The wife wanting to buy a Porsche, versus the husband who is more than happy with a Ford. They are both cars. Both vehicles move people between two points, yet they can represent contrasting things in our minds. Perhaps the Porsche represents status, personal success, and confidence to the wife. This point of view could be quite alien to the husband, who needs no such assurance. These differences in viewpoint create conflict, and while this example may be moderate in terms of impact, consider this when applied to serious or societal conflict. It's not difficult to extrapolate the car example above, for example, with a country with a totally different opinion on freedom of speech versus its citizens.

The need for the Imaginary Me to hold on to an opinion at all costs (its very existence depends on it) has been the root of almost all global conflict. Be it religious, ethical, or power-based. Simply put, *"I see it this way, I am right, and I will try to change the world outside to align with my internal opinion."*

Despite that, we all possess introspection and often see that we are wrong. We just keep going anyway. The damage we are causing by sticking to our guns is also seen through those tinted glasses and therefore feels defendable. In fact, it is the misuse of introspection that fuels this behavior due to the illusory mind being in the driver's seat. We look at ourselves through the filter of the false self and confirm we are right or have the authority to keep going, so the vicious cycle continues.

We'll see as we progress that this misalignment between the outside world "as it is" and the internal preference of the illusory mind is a major contribution to our frustration. Since the outside world is never really in our control, we tend to thrash about trying to change something that can't be changed. This thrashing causes more frustration, and the cycle continues. What we do have control of, however, is our internal state. Perhaps we balance that instead?

Perceiving Objects as Finite in Time

Consider our tendency to want to acquire things beyond the basic needs to survive (food, shelter, security, etc.). What is driving the desire for things we don't need? Is our security dependent on that tenth pair of shoes? Our physical health on the third vacation in a year? How about the multiple marital affairs or even just that

Cloudless Reality

second candy bar. I'm not saying we shouldn't want nice things. Life is here to be enjoyed. Even my dog Sadie would rather eat peanut butter than her dog food! It's not the desire for nicer things that cause us problems; it's our reaction to *not* having them. The illusory mind is fueled by the concept of lack. Primarily lack of time and lack of resources.

I confess I'm old enough to remember the Cabbage Patch Kids craze back in 1983. For some reason, these cute little dolls became a much-desired Christmas gift for kids that year. So much so that as the demand for these things far outweighed the supply, parents were fighting in toy stores over them. Obviously, they knew that was wrong and irrational, yet it happened in hundreds of toy stores worldwide. How about grocery store shelves when there's a big storm approaching? In both cases, there is a perceived lack of availability and time.

The perception that things exist for a finite period, that we have a limited time here, and the need to feed the illusory mind with objects to satisfy its feeling of lack, all conspire to legitimate negative behavior. The irony is that in the final analysis, all objects and experiences are time bound. Either the object ceases to exist (the car to the scrapyard), or the satisfaction created by its acquisition diminishes (the long-awaited new pair of shoes become just a pair of shoes after about a month). Both scenarios result in another onslaught of stories from the illusory mind to find something to replace the initial buzz of the object acquisition "before it's too late." Ultimately, the clock will run out for everyone at death. There is simply no escaping the certainty of the time-limited nature of object experience.

The ultimate example of a collective need to accumulate things in a time-limited view is seen in climate change. In our desire to have more objects, the collective illusion-driven personality continues to deplete the Earth's resources despite facts being plain to see. We acknowledge the impact but defend our inaction to fix it with the statement, "Nothing I can do about it myself; it's too big." Then go on accumulating. This is a supreme example of just how powerful the Imaginary Me is. We understand the current situation regarding climate change. Most of us accept the inevitability of its impact if unchecked, yet we, both collectively and individually, continue to do the very things that will bring that result about.

We think, *"The problem will be fixed in the future,"* but this is just another statement the illusionary self makes when there is no answer in the present. Akin to "kicking the can down the road," we seek solace in the assumed inevitability of a solution by someone else in the future. Still, as we will investigate further, the future simply doesn't exist. Only the present moment.

Time and the Imaginary Me

In Chapter 5, we'll take a crazy trip into the concept of time, discovering that the present moment is all we ever have. Since the illusory self is always either seeking or resisting, it typically needs to attach its opinions and commentary to either past events (memories) or future outcomes (expectations and "what if's?"). It tries to avoid the present moment at all costs since there are no problems

Cloudless Reality

to solve there and, therefore, no need for it to exist. Since most of us live as this self, however, life today is based primarily on thoughts and memories of the past (e.g., regrets, praise, guilt, jealousy) and projections into the future (hope, anxiety, dread, anticipation). Most of these thoughts are in the "uncontrolled thinking" category. So while you may not recognize a thought or comment in the moment as being "yours, "it is being created from some past experience deep within you.

> *Akin to "kicking the can down the road," we seek solace in the assumed inevitability of a solution by someone else in the future.*

Let's first look at those past experiences. There is much truth to the saying, "What's past is past." We can and must learn from our past experiences (that is exactly what memories are here to do), but we have no need to overly personalize past experiences and bring them to bear on the present moment. Especially if they result in a negative experience today. You are the sum of all your experiences to this point. There is no need to relive past events to fully experience yourself in this moment, but this is what most people do. Most often, as we've seen, past events are not simply recalled; they are also massively exaggerated. The memory itself is true, but it will almost always resurface in a distorted way. It is this distortion of memories that creates more angst for us. This, in turn, fuels the associated emotion, trapping it further within and increasing its strength. Let's see if this is true for you.

> Think about an experience that has stayed with you for a long time. It could be a past relationship, a traumatic event (don't focus on anything so traumatic that it causes you emotional pain), or something trivial you tend to recall often. Now really experience that feeling. Would you say it's a good feeling or a bad one? Would it be a feeling you would be rid of if you could? Think about how often this feeling comes up, what triggers it to arise, and how long it tends to last.

When I do this exercise, I strongly remember an incident that happened to me over twenty years ago. I was about to give a presentation to a few people in an office in New Jersey. I was young and quite nervous. Only six people were in the room, and one of them was my boss. As I stood up to begin the presentation, I felt embarrassed. My face turned bright red, and a wave of intense heat swept through me. I just stood there, unable to speak. One guy at the table started laughing and pointing at me, shouting, "He's frozen! Look at his face! Bright red! Hey, don't make a mess in here!"

Unfortunately, my boss was one of those laughing. I finally managed to pull myself together and continue, but that memory and its associated feelings still visit me occasionally. I often use my memories of past public speaking events to give myself a confidence push, *"You can do this; you've done this before!"* This is a great use of memory to assist us in the present and typically has no associated negative feelings.

However, I know I still have remnants of that day in New Jersey with me when triggered. I have felt that same emotional and physical reaction from twenty years ago surface when I see a stranger getting up to present. Sometimes I feel it when I see someone else merely writing a presentation or occasionally when I look at the PowerPoint icon on my Mac desktop. How insane is that?

Insane, but I'm sure you have memories that trigger emotions in much the same way. Everyone does. This is another powerful example of how the illusory self maintains its hold on us and keeps wide open the gap between the real and the false. Those exaggerated emotions serve no purpose except to make you feel bad. The good news is you can release those trapped emotions and rid yourself of those serpents of the past coming back to torment you.

Likewise, with the projection of future events. Typically tied to either dread ("what if . . .?") or anticipation ("I hope . . ."), all future events are illusory. They haven't happened yet. None of us knows the future, be it in one year or one second from now. While, again, planning is a worthwhile and necessary use of the human mind, looking to illusory future experiences to define our current emotional state is a recipe for misery. Fear of the future is possibly the most powerful and destructive emotion and is a honed skill of the illusory mind. We've seen the power of the voice to hold onto past events and bring them back highly exaggerated when triggered, but when projecting future events, this is even more powerful. Although many-fold, there are a finite number of past experiences the illusory self can use to exaggerate its commentary, but an infinite number of future events it can use. Remember, this voice is a part of you and, as such, has access to your fertile imagination. I'm sure you have experienced being presented with totally unrealistic future scenarios that often have no bearing on your current experience yet still create irrational fear or expectation—from the omnipresent fear of failing health to the expectation of winning the lottery this week. Good or bad, all this is the illusory mind desperately maintaining control of you by projecting an invented future. Whether that future is real or not makes no difference to the self.

Cornell University recently conducted a study[6] asking participants to write down their worries over an extended period. Researchers found that 85 percent of what the group worried about never happened, and of the 15 percent that did happen, 79 percent discovered they could handle the situation much better than anticipated. This means that 97 percent of what we worry about is fiction or exaggeration.

It is how much we buy into these false narratives that is a measure of how much fear or expectation we have of the future. Remember, the future doesn't exist, and the illusory stories weaved about it are unreal. French Renaissance writer Michel de Montaigne said five hundred years ago, "There were many terrible things in

Cloudless Reality

my life, and most of them never happened." When we can see these stories for what they really are, just a fictitious entity trying to keep hold of you, they start to settle down. Then there is no fear or anticipation since your mind is not seated in the future. It's always right here.

It is how much we buy into these false narratives that is a measure of how much fear or expectation we have of the future.

It seems obvious that the healthiest place to experience the real world and your real life is the present moment. Here we are free from worrisome memories of the past and false future projections. Every second spent in the present moment sends another message to the false self that you're not buying it and brings you another step closer to closing the disillusionment gap. As we move on to looking specifically at how we perceive objects, let's end this section with a quick present-moment experience.

Take a moment to get comfortable and still. Close your eyes and focus on the present moment. Regardless of what's happening, just be with it. It may be very quiet. You may hear cars passing or dogs barking in the distance. That's fine; just be with the sounds. Use all your senses to really feel the present moment. The smells, sounds, maybe tastes, how your clothes feel on your skin. Just feel yourself sinking deeper into this moment. Did you feel any disturbance inside? Any negative feelings about the past or future?

Your mind will no doubt try to pull you out of the present moment. Still, if you stick with it for just a few minutes, you may start to experience stillness as the narrative of the past and especially the future subsides, including any thoughts of "I don't have time for this meditation stuff!"

We will cover present-moment awareness in more depth in Chapters 7 and 8, but I hope you've been able to experience the power of the moment to take you out of the illusory flow and back to yourself.

How Do We Perceive Physical Objects?

A deeper dive into the current scientific view of what constitutes material things is covered later in the book. In the meantime, let's explore a major fallacy: how we are conditioned to believe what the "real world" is.

Objects are defined in our current worldview as complex constructions of individual physical particles we call matter. Obeying a strict set of natural laws, these particles arrange themselves into structures such as trees, clouds, and humans, and that is how we can perceive them. This is called the material view of reality. It is all very comfortable and familiar. It is also false.

Let's return to the only thing we ever know for sure. Our

experience. We know we experience a tree, but what our minds experience is our interpretation of a thing we have been conditioned to call a tree. We have absolutely no empirical evidence that there is an object called a tree growing outside our front porch. My view of that tree, while being similar in appearance, will be interpreted differently from how you would interpret it. The perception of that same tree will also vary significantly between, say, a dog or an ant or fungi growing on its branches. Which interpretation is the real one? Is there a real version of that tree "out there', or are there an infinite number of tree versions depending on the intelligence perceiving it? It seems quite arrogant to assume that the human view of any object is the one real view. It is estimated that there are over 8.7 billion plant and animal species on this planet,[7] each with its unique way of perceiving objects. So can we really say there is one perspective of anything?

A Hard Problem

We generally assume that perception is created inside our brains, and if reality is an arrangement of physical particles, then that is what the human brain is made from too. Hence a well-established assumption in this material view is that all our experiences are in a 3lb piece of jelly-like substance between our ears. Indeed, MRI scans of the brain do present patterns of electrical activity that are representative of some basic objects being observed. These same brain patterns are presented in any normal-functioning human brain observing the same object. Science, therefore, concludes that whenever a human brain displays a pattern of activity that

Getting Perspective

matches what has been seen as a tree, they are looking at a tree. From this comes the consequence of causation, that the viewing of the tree has caused the corresponding brain activity.

However, two things correlating doesn't necessarily mean that one causes the other, "correlation does not equal causation." For example, if you look at monthly ice cream sales and monthly shark attacks in the US each year, you will find that these two activities are highly correlated. Does this then mean that eating ice cream causes shark attacks? Obviously not, but correlation versus causation does create problems when we come to more nuanced relationships, such as the link between brain activity and perception. Did the tree cause brain activity? Or did a trigger in the brain create a pattern of activity that caused the observer to see what they would label as a tree? As we shall see in Chapter 6, there is a very close relationship between subject and object in observation.

Physical objects such as trees aren't the only things we experience. How about thoughts and emotions? Again, since all perception is believed to be in the brain, thoughts and emotions must also be created and experienced in the same place. Neuroscience has had great success correlating brain activity to some aspects of visual perception, as we discussed above but has been much less effective at correlating thoughts and emotions. Since these aspects of our experience are much more subjective than physical objects, they have proven more challenging to match to predictable brain activity. Some basic correlations have been seen in simple tasks such as thinking of the color red, where predictable brain patterns have been seen across multiple subjects upon thinking "red," similarly with emotions. We have seen a basic level of correlation between the feeling of, for example, fear and specific activity in the amygdala.

However, when it comes to perceiving an object, and especially with thoughts and feelings, there is far more to them than objective brain activity. Seeing the color red, for example, will solicit some emotion associated with it, which in turn may trigger a thought. None of these events have been detected in MRI scans. Moreover, the brain activity correlations don't indicate where and how our subjectivity arises. As yet, we have no idea where the subjective feeling of love arises from within the material cells of the brain, for example. Or even the subjective feeling of red. We're attempting to reduce an emotional experience to a series of data points that relate to our overall perception. As we know, there is far more to "seeing" a tree than merely seeing a tree.

This brings about what has been labeled by philosopher David Chalmers in the 1990s as the "hard problem of consciousness."[8] In short, where does the *feeling* of red come from? What is the source of the *feeling* of being in love? Can we replicate those experiences in the brain? Despite decades of looking for solid causation of even basic thoughts and feelings within the brain, we have made little progress. There is no scientific evidence that thoughts and emotions, and I would argue the interpretation of anything more than very simple physical objects, can be created solely by electrical impulses generated from neurons in the human brain. Indeed, we have seen no evidence anywhere in the universe where consciousness itself has been generated from physical matter.

There is ample evidence, however, to believe the brain serves as a control hub for many aspects of the human body. If certain parts of the brain are damaged, for example, we know the impact that damage will have on bodily and psychological function. There are, however, many other aspects of brain function that we simply have no answer to in our current worldview. The prevailing scientific response to this situation is along the lines of a promissory note. That we will figure out at some future point in time where in the brain the feeling of fear, for example, is located. It is necessary to continue along this path since the question of how we experience anything is fundamental to us as a species. We should, however, also be open to considering other views of reality that abrogate the hard problem of consciousness as we shall see in the next chapter.

If we agree that all we know of anything is our experience of it, and if we cannot say for certain that the source of experience is in the brain (or anywhere in the body, for that matter), then we have a fundamental problem with our current worldview. There is evidently something else going on here. If we cannot categorically say that subjective experiences happen in the body, where do they happen?

Understanding What Things Are

One of the reasons we have stalled on this foundational point in our understanding of ourselves is the method used to investigate experience. It is assumed in mainstream science that the observer and the thing being observed are independent of each other. When we look at an object, there is an observer of the object and the object itself—two discrete systems. This fundamental assumption works extremely well for most scientific investigations. If we observe the mating habits of puffins, we are a set of human eyes observing the birds and gaining valuable knowledge and insights from this. The birds are separate objects in time and space, and we can observe them without impacting us (the observers).

However, when we come to observe our own internal experiences, we are observing the very act of our observing. This creates a complication in that we cannot observe our own experiences without being part of the experience. The act of observation impacts our observation because we are the ones observing! Hope I haven't lost you. It is impossible to know that our experiences result in a certain pattern of activity in a brain scanner because observing the brain scan is itself an experience.

A popular misconception of science is that it describes what things *are*. The truth is that the scientific method was created to describe the way things *behave* so that we can predict future events. Science has proved extremely effective in this regard, resulting in some extraordinary feats of achievement. However, when you think more deeply about some of the major scientific discoveries through the ages (gravity, thermodynamics, relativity, quantum mechanics, etc.), we are describing predictable behaviors and not the thing in itself.

Probably the best example of this is our understanding of the basic building blocks of reality as assumed in the material view. Once thought to be the fundamental level of matter, the atom has since been deconstructed until we now have several competing theories as to what it is. Although we can't explicitly see these building blocks, we can see interactions of what we assume is a solid piece of matter via interactions with other assumed pieces of matter. It is through these interactions that science has created a theory for the structure of the atom, consisting of a nucleus of neutrons and protons, with each atom having a specific number of electrons orbiting this nucleus. The size of these three sub-atomic constituents, and the relative distance of the electrons from the atomic nucleus, gives rise to the conclusion drawn experimentally in 1911 by Ernest Rutherford, that atoms are mostly empty space. To be more precise, 99.9999999999996 percent empty space. Hence the "matter" we observe as objects, including ourselves, is, to all intents and purposes, empty. Yet when we look at objects, we perceive them as solid things. What we perceive when we look at

Rather than separate and distinct "things," the only truth we can claim about objects we perceive is that we really do perceive them.

anything is a reconstruction of the thing "out there" by our brain "in here." We never see the object in itself (if we did, it looks like we'd see almost nothing!). Likewise, we never hear, touch, smell, or taste anything as it is, only how we construct it internally.

As we can see, it doesn't take long for cracks to appear in our traditional consideration of how we experience our reality. Since it appears that the brain may not be the exclusive storehouse of experience, then we must ask ourselves, "What is?" The fact that we experience anything means that something is going on here. We just don't have a line of sight to what that is in the material worldview. So maybe this worldview isn't the right one. Rather than separate and distinct "things," the only truth we can claim about objects we perceive is that we really do perceive them.

The Vicious Cycle

In this chapter, we have investigated a few aspects of the current worldview and their impact on us, individually and collectively. Today most of us are living as an illusory self that thrives on being separate from others and from the world. This persona has a definite (albeit subjective) view of what that world is that it defends vigorously. It has an insatiable need for objects and experience accumulation and lives primarily in the past or the future.

The influence of the illusory mind is fueled by its belief in what reality is. When we look at the main characteristics of the illusory self and the current material view of reality, we can see some striking similarities. This shouldn't be surprising since the two have evolved in unison. Let's look at some supporting views of the material view of reality and the illusory mind. We can see, when we look at just three examples, how the material view and the illusory mind tend to feed each other through their views.

Example 1
Material View
The world is made from individual particles of matter. All objects, from stars to humans, are collections of these particles, and so are themselves individual and separate.

Illusory Self
Since everything is separate, then we need to protect this individual from possible harm from other separate things.

Example 2
Material View
The entirety of our human experience is contained within the brain, a complex arrangement of particles. There's nothing special about how we experience our world. Experiences are electrical impulses we haven't worked out how to decode yet.

Illusory Self
We're akin to sophisticated machines, where our deepest thoughts and experiences can be reduced to signals. Our purpose must therefore be to pass on our genes. Beyond that, life doesn't need meaning.

Example 3
Material View
Since we are purely material beings, we are born, we live our lives, and then we die. Nothing is preserved. This is a mechanistic world that has its rules.

Illusory Self
We'll be here for about eighty years. When we die, we are rather akin to a robot being deactivated. Other than

short-lived memories of our loved ones and lineage, our impact on the world will probably be minuscule.
We might as well get as much out of these eighty years as possible. After that, it's gone for good.

Distortions of the Illusory Self

As you can see, rather like a reinforcing cycle, the material worldview provides a safe harbor for an illusory self, validating its own physical worldview through introspection. Since the illusory mind is wholly responsible for our negative feelings, is it any wonder that most people are experiencing either a constant undercurrent of unease, frequently spiking into severe unhappiness, or are in a chronic state of misery and anxiety? We have only to look around with our current material worldview glasses on to see that what the illusory mind is saying makes some sense. This isn't our natural state. It's a state that has evolved through the cycle of reinforcement of a false self in a material-centric world. Until we see this world differently, we can't understand this illusion and hence reduce its impact on us.

Although we're painting a rather grim picture of today's worldview, we must remember that the human mind is an awesome gift of nature. With our ability to introspect, we are capable and have achieved great things. There is no reason why we can't explore new ways of looking at reality yet retain this ability to create, discover and construct natural laws regarding how the world works. Remember, we were the ones who created this material worldview and its accompanying illusory self. We can also get ourselves out of them.

The material worldview is just one step in the evolution of human consciousness. We have much more to contribute to our society and to the planet, but we must evolve past this way of looking at the world. It's time to consider an alternative view based only on what we, as conscious beings, can verify through direct experience. One in which the illusory me is placed into context and where your true self can thrive. That is where we find our meaning in life. Trust me, this alternative view differs greatly from what you may think! That is the topic of the next chapter.

Chapter 3

The Human Experience

Is Reality Just One Big Experience?

In Chapter 2, we examined aspects of the prevailing material view of the world and investigated some of the consequences of that worldview. Based on the assumption that the material world is the foundational layer of our experience, we can see how this serves to fuel the influence of the illusory mind. If the world is seen as separate and distinct objects, including humans, where time is a scarce resource and the present moment is merely a means to get to an imaginary future, then our illusory self is reinforced. Since we understand this illusion to be the source of much of our discomfort and dissatisfaction, to reduce its influence, we must re-examine the way we view the world.

Perceiving Reality Through Direct Experience

Over the next couple of chapters, let's leave the illusory self for a while and look more deeply into how we perceive reality. We'll do some exploring based only on our direct experience and, leaving assumptions behind, develop an alternative worldview based on intuition. The current material worldview has been successfully constructed based on a predictive model. As such, it is primarily objective in nature. This has given rise to a tremendous ability to predict but has left us short in understanding what things really are and where our experiences come from. We know that our experience (again, the only thing we know for sure exists) is mostly subjective. So, let's see what happens when we take a more subjective view of our world.

So far, we've referred to three types of human experience—objects, thoughts, and feelings. Outside of these experiences, we have no empirical evidence that anything exists in its own right. When you see something, you only know we see it because you experience it within you. The same goes for any of your five senses. Your thoughts and feelings are very much a part of your inner world too. Although no one else can access these, we know they are very real to us.

Maybe take a moment to verify that this is true for you: that life only consists of experiences based on the things you sense, the thoughts you have, and the emotions you feel. This is the basis of our subjective exploration to follow.

Are Objects Real?

How we perceive physical objects is one of the most misunderstood types of experience. Let's drill into that a little more here and consider what an object really is.

Most of us today look at a door and believe there is an object called a door, about 10ft away from us, that opens and closes to

Cloudless Reality

let us in and out of the room. What's more, if there was someone with us in the room, they would see the exact same door in the same place, performing the same function. That's great. It helps us navigate the world and interact with others. Unfortunately, the truth is there is no door. There is just a concept of a door that has been agreed upon by the collective human psyche. I know that sounds far-fetched, but bear with me, and you'll see how this is an obvious truth based purely on our experience.

To start, take a moment and think about what makes an object an object.

Most people own a car. A car is an object we perceive as having four wheels, a cabin, an engine (or electric motor), windows, doors, a trunk, a hood, and numerous other things we collectively define as a car.

Imagine your car or any car. Now let's take away the wheels. Is it still a car? Most would say yes, it is. You can't get far in it, but it is still a car. Okay, how about we take out the engine and the doors. Still a car? Well, yes, but it's missing a few vital parts.

How many things would you have to take away from the car until it would cease to be called a car? Isn't a car just a collection of other objects arranged in such a way that we have collectively agreed is a car? If you took all the parts used to construct a car, threw them up in the air, and let them fall on the ground, would that still be a car?

Feel free to do this with any physical object, even your body (although that may be gross!).

If you did the above exercise, you now know that you can apply this to any object. A table with no legs? Well, some tables have no legs. A flat surface suspended from the ceiling with cables could be considered a table. How about the utility of the object? If you can place a cup of coffee on a flat surface, then that flat surface must be a table . . . unless it's the hood of your car. So where are we going with this?

Basically, when we try to define any object, it can only be understood as a "something" because we have collectively decided it is so and educated others to understand it that way too. At some point in the distant past, someone invented a thing that we now call a table, and that information has been passed down through generations. If you have kids, you probably told them early on that that strange-looking structure in the middle of the room with four legs wasn't about to walk over to them but was actually a thing called a "table" that you put things on.

When we remove the blinders of conditioning, we see a table is just a series of other objects or shapes brought together to form something we have all agreed to call a table. We could equally call it "a horizontal cuboid with four vertically oriented cuboids of equal length located at each corner," but that would be a mouthful! If we each perceived what we call a table in a completely

Cloudless Reality

different way, society would cease to function as we would have no common rules of communication; we would all be speaking our own discrete language.

If you think about a table or any object you can perceive, rather than a collection of other objects that constitute the overall object, you'll find you tend to perceive the "feeling" of the object instead. When you look at a table, you just "know" it's a table, or a cup, or a human, or a spiral galaxy. This is how we were able to collectively evolve. If we had to understand that the object moving toward us with fur, four legs, big teeth, and hungry-looking eyes was a lion about to pounce, we'd soon be extinct. It's a more effective survival strategy to look at the lion as "lion = danger" and instantly make the necessary survival moves. The same goes for any object we sense. After a certain age, we tend to intuitively know what most things are rather than having to decode their constituent parts.

When we try to define any object, it can only be understood as a "something" because we have collectively decided it is so and educated others to understand it that way too.

We call this "feeling" of an object its "essence', as originally coined by the fourth century BCE philosopher Plato, or what Hindus would call the "dharma" of an object. A car with no wheels, doors, or engine still retains the essence of a car. So, we perceive the world as subjective "essences," or to put it another way, experiences. Not objective things.

This subjective view of things helps explain how objects are experienced by our non-human friends. A bee will see a flower very differently from us. Neither the bee nor the human will see a flower as a complex combination of photosynthesizing molecules. Humans would experience the flower's essence as a beautiful plant with attractive petals and a pleasant aroma. The bees would see the flower as food. All are just subjective experiences.

How can you sense the essence of objects? Try this . . .

> Consider the book you're reading—on paper or a device. If you look at this physical book, can you say with any doubt that that book exists? Where is the book? In your hand? Really think about this. How do you know the book is there? For that matter, how do you know your hand is there holding the book? Look around the room at objects you see. How do you know they are really there? Ultimately aren't the book, your hand, and the room all experienced in your mind?

We are taught that light from the sun, or artificial light, bounces off an object, hits your retina, converts the light to electrical signals in your optic nerve, and heads to the brain, where the signals are decoded into your subjective experience of a book. The book, as you experience it, is merely a sequence of electrical signals in the brain that can formulate an image and a "feel" of a book based on prior conditioning. The current materialist belief is that there is an object out there separate from you, but it can only be perceived as a book in the brain. We can never know what is resting in your hand since it is always viewed through interpretation, never directly.

In fact, any object we perceive is more like a reconstruction of what comes into our senses based on prior conditioning rather than a physical object in front of us. We see the world as a combination of five types of sensations: namely sight, sound, smell, taste, and touch. It just so happens that the "real world" we see also consists of things made up of these five sensations. Either that is a monumental coincidence, or we perceive only what our senses can pick up and construct a world inside us based on those senses.

This way of explaining how we perceive objects is called "materialism."[9] The theory is that we experience the world in our brains, but the source of this experience is a physical world outside it. In our example, materialism states that the book exists as a collection of particles in your hand, but you cannot experience them directly. You experience the book inside the brain as information comes in through your senses. In that regard, any object you can possibly perceive is only ever experienced in the brain. Effectively, one collection of matter (book) causes a reaction in another piece of matter (brain), resulting in experience.

Although this theory seems to make sense in how we experience objects via our senses, it suffers from some weaknesses, a few of which we've already discussed. First, it assumes that there is something "out there" called a book from which your senses can pick up information. If our internal experience is all we know,

The Human Experience

how can we say unambiguously that there is something in your hand in the first place? If you dreamed of holding a book, your experience would be the same, but there wouldn't be an actual book there. So, you already have some evidence that you don't need to be holding matter to experience holding a book. All we ever experience is the subjective feeling of a thing we call a book.

Second, the theory assumes that the brain receives this incoming information and decodes it according to prior conditioning into something that has the essence of a book. As we've previously discussed, however, there is more to an object than its raw physicality. You may have a very different type of "book" experience from me, although we are reading the same one. We know from the hard problem of consciousness that we have no evidence of this type of subjective experience generated in the brain. This seems even more improbable when we take the book example and expand that to anything we could possibly perceive. From earthworms to neutron stars and everything in between, materialism would have it that we experience all that within a human brain. I'm not saying the brain isn't capable; it just feels unintuitive that that would be the case.

As you'll see, materialism has proved an effective steppingstone to a more complete picture of reality, as it concedes the fact that we have no proof of what's really "out there." All we can ever know is what's "in here." Materialism maintains, however, that there *is* a physical world outside of your brain that causes these internal experiences. Although we can't see this world for what it really is, we can measure it precisely using instruments and mathematics.

Cloudless Reality

We know how long something is, how heavy it is, how fast it is etc. By assigning units of measurement to the things we experience situated outside of us, we have constructed a very effective map of the world. The map, however, is not the real world. We can't measure the weight of a thought, the speed of an emotion, or the energy of a thought. Yet these are a substantial part of our experience of physical objects.

Since we've found that objects can only be perceived as subjective experiences, how about the other two sources of experiences we're aware of? Thoughts and feelings are undoubtedly experiences that we perceive within ourselves; they are not outside of us. We interpret thoughts and feelings as much as we interpret physical objects within us. There is something that feels fearful, happy, or sad, just like there is an "essence" to a table. In fact, the subjective experience of any physical object is usually associated with a thought or feeling. We could conclude that this subjective experience of an object is the same subjective experience as a thought or a feeling. They are just different types of experiences. And since objects, thoughts, and feelings are all we can ever know, and all we ever know is our experience, then it seems logical to assume that:

Reality = Experience

Think about this statement for a second. There are multiple levels of insight here. Again, based only on your experience, objects you perceive, thoughts you think, and emotions you feel are all *only* subjective experiences. Since we cannot prove there is any physical world "out there," then *everything* is experience. We're

The Human Experience

now stepping beyond materialism to claim that the book you're reading is not a physical object in space that you reconstruct internally. We're claiming the book itself and the essence of the book, as perceived, are all experiential. The book in your hand, the room you sit in now, and even your hand don't consist of external matter. They are all experiences of your mind in *exactly* the same way your thoughts and feelings are. Not all in *your*

> *Since objects, thoughts, and feelings are all we can ever know, and all we ever know is our experience, it seems logical to assume that: Reality = Experience.*

mind, not all in *my* mind, but *of* mind. If all we can experience is what happens in our minds, then maybe all that anyone ever experiences is a broader mind? Perhaps the world is actually made from mind stuff and not material stuff? Stay with me.

If everything consists of perceptions in mind, then how can we say for sure there is any difference between, say, my seeing my pet dog in my mind and seeing my dog sat snoring in a chair in front of me right now? The truth is, we can't prove that there is any difference. It's in this way that we can begin to understand curious observations in nature, such as the placebo effect, where a mental state in a patient can cause a 'physical' effect in their bodies that brings about healing. Both the thought and the healing are in mind.

We've just laid the foundation for a new view of the world. The claim above may seem difficult to grasp. It was for me until I began to experience it for myself. So, spend a couple of minutes sensing this singular experience.

Cloudless Reality

Give yourself a few minutes to get comfortable, relax your body, maybe take a few deep breaths, and close your eyes. Now focus on anything you are currently feeling through your senses. The feeling of the chair beneath you, the air on your skin, any noise you can hear, any smells or tastes you can detect. Really focus on anything you can sense "externally."

Okay, now focus on **where** you sense those experiences. Are you sensing the feeling of the air literally on your skin? The noise of passing cars literally at those cars, or maybe even your ears? If you really dive deep, what you'll hopefully find is that all these sensations are happening in one place. It doesn't matter for now where that place is; the important thing is they are all happening in the same place. If you go deep enough, you may sense that they are all one thing.

Do the same for any thoughts or feelings that come up. Where are you experiencing them? In your head, your heart, your stomach? When you get past the visceral feeling of them, you may find that the answer to this investigation is the same as the physical senses. They all seem to be happening in the same place.

Finally, combine your experience of senses, thoughts,

and feelings. Let whatever arises just come to you. Again, try to find the places where these experiences are being individually felt. You may find that there is only one thing here. Again, don't try to figure out what that is. The important thing is that these experiences seem to come together at one point.

Hopefully, you'll start to sense something akin to a point, or maybe a void, where you perceive all these experiences. Regardless of the experience, it feels like it's happening in the same place. The place itself is difficult to locate, and that's not important right now, but I hope you've sensed where all experience is perceived. We'll see in the truth of our new reality that where these experiences arise is the same as where the observer we've talked about previously resides.

Meeting the Observer

You met the concept of the observer, "I," in Chapter 1. Hopefully, from the exercise above, you've been able to intuit a single source of experience. If everything we perceive are mental experiences, then how do we know we are perceiving them? Who is the one doing the perceiving?

We unambiguously know that we experience things. If not, we wouldn't even be here (or rather, we wouldn't know that we were here!). The seventeenth-century philosopher Rene Descartes is famous for saying, "I think, therefore I am." I don't believe that is strictly true. We don't have to think about something to experience it. How about the first amazing sunset your saw or the first time you fell in love. They were powerful experiences, but you probably weren't thinking much then. In fact, it was a lack of thinking that allowed the experience to arise. I'd rather upgrade Descartes' statement to, "You *experience*, therefore you exist," or better still, "You are *aware* that you experience, therefore you exist."

We know we experience objects (tables, cars, pugs, other people), thoughts (that typically have either a vocal or visual element to them), and emotions (typically having a physical component to them). These three types of experience are often interconnected. For example, I think of an object (a boat) that causes me to think about a memory of being on a cruise vacation a few years back that fills me with happiness. Likewise, I can think about how much I love my daughter, and from that emotion and those thoughts comes an image of playing hockey with her in the park at the weekend. Nothing special about these experiences; they are a natural part of our lives.

Although natural, how can we see the connections between these experiences but not be in the experience itself? It's almost like we are watching the activities of experience, like watching a movie on a screen. We intuit that these experiences arise from the same location, so it seems there is a sort of centralized and independent observer of those experiences individually and as an interconnected whole. Someone is watching the movie.

Back in Chapter 1, we touched on the existence of the observer of our experiences. Now it's time to delve into the nature of this awareness. It's nothing short of one of the most important insights; let's break it down.

We know that we cannot possibly be the objects we perceive. When we see a chair, we don't say, "I am that chair." We say, "I see that chair," or "I experience that chair."

> *If everything we perceive is mental experiences, then how do we know we are perceiving them? Who is the one doing the perceiving?*

As stated in Chapter 1, you know from science that our physical body is almost wholly replaced every hundred days. If you are your physical body, then you must change all the time. Do you feel like this happens? How about if you lost your arms, your legs, your liver? Even your heart and lungs can be replaced with a machine. Would that change *you*? Who *are you*? What *you* experience?

Our thoughts come and go like the wind, mostly (as we've seen) not under our control. In Chapter 1, we referred to intense nervousness before standing to speak publicly being absent after the speech, so emotions are also mostly transient and, again, mostly not under our control. Does it *feel* (excuse the pun) intuitive to say we *are* our thoughts or emotions?

Yet despite all this change in what we experience, there seems to be a constant knowing of "me." We can make the statements above only because we have experienced them all. From your personal experience, I'm sure it seems that there is someone "in there" that is aware of what you experience but is not "of" those things you experience. Whoever it is has been a constant

Cloudless Reality

throughout your entire life. Indeed, it is the one thing we can say for certain doesn't change. This is what we call "I."

If you are aware of only objects, thoughts, and emotions, yet you are none of these, then you must be the one who is aware of them.

The core truth of life is that if you are aware of only objects, thoughts, and emotions, yet you are none of these, then you must be the one who is aware of them. You are not the movie, you are the audience that watches the movie. I think this is the most liberating knowledge we possess. When you can step back in the face of emotional events and occupy the observer role, you don't get so invested in life's dramas anymore. This awareness is the ground state of our reality and, as I've previously hinted at, is no less than what the universe is.

Let's take an excursion to meet this awareness personally.

Think of a thought or a feeling. It can be anything. Now ask yourself, who knows you're having that thought or feeling? Don't expect to get an explicit answer to this question. It's meant to provide just a sense of the "me" who is watching.

Now cast your mind back to when you were a teenager and do the same thing. Now go back as far as you can remember and do the same thing. I find it helps to imagine looking into a mirror at each stage and seeing into the eyes of the reflection of the "me" beneath.

Then, ask yourself the following two questions.
- Was the physical person, their thoughts, and their emotions the same in all three cases?
- Is the sense of "me" the same in all three cases?

Hopefully, you've just experienced that although your body, thoughts, feelings, and emotions change over time, you sense an awareness that stays the same. Did you get a sense of who that "me" was? Where was it? Don't worry, that's not easy.

Since we live in a world of subject-object, it's very difficult to find words to describe the one thing that is neither (since everything happens within it). You can feel its presence when you ask, *"Am I aware right now?"* Immediately you ask yourself that question, see how your mental activity subsides while your mind tries to find an answer. It can't. The answer to that question lies in awareness itself. Only awareness can be aware of itself.

When we say "I am sad," we typically focus on the "sad" part of that statement. We seldom ponder the meaning of the "I" part, do we? If we asked someone in the street what they mean by "I," they would probably respond by saying something along the lines of (as we did in Chapter 2), "I'm a middle-aged woman with a good job and nice house living in France." Again, is that who you *really* are?

There is something much deeper to this "I" than describing your life's current or past situations. Something that is not transient. It's also something that is at once familiar yet elusive. Let's try a different way to sense it.

Think of something that makes you happy. It could be a friend, your partner, your pet, or anything that puts a smile on your face. Think to yourself, "I am happy." Now ask yourself what is the "I" that is happy? Try to find it. Try to describe it. I don't mean label it as anything; just find it. Visualize it. Does it have a shape, a weight, a color, or a size?

Difficult, right? Yet that "I" is how we label ourselves every day.

Now do the same things as above but think of something that makes you unhappy or triggers an emotion that is not wanted. Now ask yourself again, "Who is the "I" that is having this experience?" Try to find it.

The exercise above is called "self-inquiry" and is a powerful way to sense more of the real nature of awareness. We'll speak more of this in Chapter 8, so don't worry if you didn't find a clear sense of "I" here because you're not supposed to. The exercise aims to help you look past the "I" label to the "I" itself and find nothing tangible.

During my own self-inquiries, most often during meditation, I'm tracing my way from an emotion-based "I am x" statement ("I am cold," for example) to try to find the "I" that is aware of that emotion. Although I don't find an explicit answer, I sense something akin to spaciousness, lightness, an expanse of some kind, rather like the sky.

What's more, when I inquire into other "I" statements that are not just emotion centered, such as "I am in my living room," "I am human," "I'm thinking of my car," and again look to trace the "I," I inevitably end up at the same place as when I was tracing an emotion.

What I've gleaned in this self-inquiry exercise is that the location where thoughts, feelings, and perceptions are experienced and where I find the observer doing the experiencing is the *same place*. Ultimately there is only one place, awareness. As we'll see, this is not just my personal awareness but the universal awareness we are all a part of. How would *you* describe what this awareness is?

> *The key to liberation is rediscovering this awareness by clearing away whatever obscures it.*

At best, I can say it's timeless, changeless, peaceful, and infinite, but even those words don't paint an accurate picture. Buddhists call it the void, Hindus call it Krishna, Christians call it God, and others call it the universe or source. As we'll see in Chapter 6, science often uses the label "Quantum Field." Simply put, it is "I," and it is who you really are. The reason why we don't all live with this awareness is that it's been hidden. The key to liberation is rediscovering this awareness by clearing away whatever obscures it.

Cloudless Reality

A Cloudless Sky

When I lived in the UK, I used to visit the Lake District, a popular National Park, as often as I could. I'm an avid hillwalker, sometimes dabbling in rock climbing, and I love getting away from it all to get to an elevation. Something in me craved spaciousness, the feeling of being on top of the world, closer to the sky. I vividly remember walking the Langdale Pikes (beautiful peaks with a glacial lake, Stickle Tarn, at the top) and lying on the grass, looking up at the blue sky. I remember thinking how lucky I was to be looking up at a blue, sun-filled sky since that part of the country didn't often experience that kind of day.

As I lay back and looked up, I noticed several fluffy white clouds pass between me and the sun, temporarily casting a shadow. I remember feeling disappointed that my bathing in rare English sunlight was temporarily halted due to a cloud. After a few seconds, the cloud passed by, and I returned to my sunlit bliss once more. I didn't realize it then, but this experience would stay with me as a powerful metaphor for how to live my life. Let me explain.

The awareness that is the real you and that, as we've discussed, is unchanging, constant, and always present is akin to the blue sky I was engrossed in on that mountain. The clouds that move across the sky are akin to objects, thoughts, and emotions that move across awareness. They temporarily hide the blue sky, but they never affect it. Regardless of how many clouds come across the sky, that sky is always there. Regardless of how many and how severe the clouds are that move across the real you, that true self can never be impacted by them, only temporarily hidden. I hope that analogy makes sense to you because it is one of the important messages of this book. Your authentic self is the sky. It is *not* the clouds that pass by. Unfortunately, however, most people literally live "in the clouds."

Our lives represent the combination of the sky and clouds. The sky wouldn't be the sky without the occasional cloud. The beauty of the world is that it is always in motion. Life would be boring and unchallenging if we had continuous blue skies (although anyone in the northern hemisphere might disagree!). What I'm trying to say is that the clouds that come across the sky are a necessary part of life. Some may be merely whisps that pass almost unnoticed (a dog barking in the distance). Some just stay a few minutes ("I just stubbed my toe, and it hurts. How could I be so careless!"). Then there are those huge thunderclouds that can stick around for months or years ("She wants to divorce me, I'm worthless.").

> *Your authentic self is the sky. It is not the clouds that pass by.*

As with the weather, our lives unfold according to natural laws we have little control over. There will be periods of sun and days of cloud. Times of drizzle, times of downpour. Obviously, no one really wants hours of torrential rain, but if that's the weather that day, it is what it is. Just as we can't change the weather, we can't change what the world will throw at us at any given time. You might say the secret to moving closer to your true self is to be okay with the weather, whatever it is.

Cloudless Reality

Most of the time, it's pointless trying to change your external circumstances to avoid a cloud, yet this is what most people do. "I'm not going to that party because people won't talk to me." Or how about, "I can't believe it's raining on my wedding day. It's unfair!" There are far more things in life you can't change than you can, yet most people's reaction to negative situations is to try to change them because they don't align with what they want inside, and their "inside" must be right. This is akin to trying to change the weather to the forecast you prefer. It takes a huge amount of effort and ultimately isn't possible! Since there is only ever one version of a situation happening at any time, it's simply impossible for everyone to have their own happy version of what the world is doing. We all just need to be okay with the weather; it's that simple. Who is it that's complaining about the weather? You guessed it, our old pal, the illusory mind. The source of every raincloud you will ever experience.

Before we dive into cloud control (see what I did there?), I'd like to elaborate on the experiences we're dealing with here. I'm talking primarily about irrational psychological experiences. Those experiences are unnecessary and serve no purpose. If your current experience requires a change in the situation (you're crossing the road, and a car is coming), we all have an innate intelligence that will take over and get you out of the situation. These events aren't typically the causes of our discontent. What makes us uneasy and frustrated are the illusory mind-born experiences that have no need to stay in our cognition.

Managing Clouds

I hope you are starting to see that the key to a more complete life can never be found in trying to fix your outside situation when things don't "go your way." It is all about managing the clouds that pass by. Rather than frantically trying to change the world to align with what feels good inside, look inward and align from there. Then you align yourself with the weather, and from there, things get a lot easier. When you can manage your response to the clouds, regardless of their size and duration, your outside circumstances align with your true self, and there is no unease. The root of the feeling of incompleteness and lack of purpose we experience, the source of the big questions that plague us, is simply the masking of the blue sky by all the clouds that pass by. In that sky are completeness, happiness, and your purpose in life; it is you!

According to the National Science Foundation, 80 percent of our thoughts are negative, and 95 percent are repetitive. Given we have about 60,000 thoughts per day,[10] that's a lot of clouds scuttling past our cognition daily. Many of these simply pass without a reaction from us. Objects, such as signposts when you're driving to work. Thoughts ("I like that dress") and emotions ("I love this brand of coffee!") are mostly just observed and then leave. They evaporate

> *The root of the feeling of incompleteness and lack of purpose we experience, the source of the big questions that plague us, is simply the masking of the blue sky by all the clouds that pass by. In that sky are completeness, happiness, and your purpose in life; it is you!*

into the atmosphere as clouds naturally do. While they may stay in your memory for a while, they don't cause a reaction, nor do they obscure the sky for more than a few seconds. But what about the clouds that don't get through?

These are those negative thoughts and emotions that solicit a reaction from your mind. These are the clouds you likely hold back. They are typically high-voltage emotions that your mind stores away for future use, just as in the "Rose and Thorn" story from Chapter 2. Here is that story again, broken down into what's happening in the landscape of the mind.

You look at a rose; it is the most amazing thing you've ever seen. The bright red petals, the feel of the stem, the beautiful aroma, just wonderous.

Awareness observes the rose directly, with no emotion or thought attached. This is how we're supposed to experience the world. The sky is clear.

As you look at the rose, you prick your thumb on a thorn. That was not what you expected. It caused surprise, pain, a feeling of unpredictability, and a threat to your security. You even see drops of blood on your finger.

There is a misalignment between what was expected and what the world did. A dark cloud has appeared, and the sky has been obscured.

Hysterical, you drop the rose and run to tell your parents what happened. Unfortunately, your parents tell you that roses can be very dangerous due to their thorns and that the prick on your finger must be cleaned immediately; otherwise, it could get infected and hurt even more and for longer.

The Human Experience

Misalignment has been reinforced by authority. The mind can't let that cloud just pass by. This is serious, so you hold onto it.

You now fear, maybe even hate, roses—and may do for the rest of your life.

The emotion is unnaturally trapped. You didn't let it go. That cloud now permanently occupies a part of the sky. It may lie dormant most of the time, but if you see another rose, maybe even another flower, it will expand again, just like a growing thunderstorm. Like a thunderstorm, the cloud will grow to a size way beyond the original cloud. This is the irrational exaggeration of past emotions by the illusory mind we experienced earlier.

Can you see how this scenario is so common? It's repeated countless times until, for some people, they simply stop seeing any part of the sky. This is depression. This is why people abuse drugs. This is the source of suicide. Regardless of who you are and what you have done, you have an authentic self, and it *is* that sky. When you lose sight of the sky completely, you are lost. The reason why people turn to radical ways to "get high", is literally to get back up to that beautiful blue sky again. People engage in extreme sports so that when they can't focus on anything at the moment other than survival, those illusory clouds move away, albeit temporarily.

This may sound daunting but trust me when I say it is possible to clear the sky of those dark clouds you've been holding on to. The first step is to understand the dynamics of the sky and the clouds, get to know the mechanics of the illusory mind, then start cleaning out the clouds to feel that sun on your face again.

Cloudless Reality

Changing Perspectives

If you understand the concept of the watcher of your thoughts and feelings, you're halfway there. Spend as much time as you can as this independent watcher. When you feel angry, rather than think, "I am angry" (which cannot be true!), rather think, "I can see that [*insert your name*] is feeling the emotion of anger." Can you see the change in perspective? Subtle but extremely powerful. It is the same for positive emotions too. The more time you spend in this "seat of consciousness," the more you will naturally start to clear away the clouds. It's almost as though the sky is pushing them away, so you can see more of it.

In this chapter, we explored the nature of reality as an experience and investigated who is the one experiencing it all. As we continue our excursion into an experienced-based world model, let's now look at the nature of this reality and what it means to life and meaning. I hope you're sitting comfortably. This next chapter is a doozy.

Chapter 4

Life in the Whirlpool
So What Does Reality Really Look Like?

We've drilled into some detail about the experiential nature of reality and the "I," the awareness of it all. Now let's take that a little further. Let's examine the common experience of this awareness and expand that to the world beyond the personal. There seems to be an underlying commonality to how we experience the world, even though our personal world is inaccessible to anyone else. We know what is happening in the vicinity of our perception but have no idea what's happening beyond that. We all agree on what a flower is, although we differ in the emotions that arise on looking at that flower. So, why is the world like this? How come we have personal awareness anyway, and how does all this relate to life and purpose? We'll explore these points to see that the nature of this personal and shared awareness is intimately tied to our happiness and our purpose in life.

Pure Awareness

Remember that basing what is real purely on experience leads

Cloudless Reality

us to the unambiguous conclusion that we experience only three things:

1. Objects in the world.
2. Thoughts about the world.
3. Feelings of the world.

The analogy of the sky and the clouds can help us understand how we hold on to emotionally charged experiences, be they from an object, a thought, or a feeling. We've also investigated the "I" as the observer that is aware of everything that is. And from the excursions in the previous chapter, you've likely sensed that it's very difficult to answer the "Who am I?" question. This is true for everyone, from the person on the street to the sages of Tibet. However, if pushed, we tend to use the same description across the board. Infinite, vast, spacious, peaceful, stable, secure, constant, empty, untouchable, void.

> *The analogy of the sky and the clouds can help us understand how we hold on to emotionally charged experiences, be they from an object, a thought, or a feeling.*

Staying just with our experience, let's consider some common characteristics of the "I."

- Everyone tends to describe it in the same way.
- We all have a common desire for happiness. It may be represented differently (job, house, car, power, relationship, health), but everyone has a root drive—to be happy.
- Descriptions of objects, feelings, and emotions are often similar for many people.

- We can see most people have an ego, or illusory self, just by interacting with them.
- Regardless of who we are, we all have a deep-seated desire for connection to others.
- People often describe a similar experience when the mind is quiet (amazing sunset, falling in love, scaling a rock wall).

We teased out earlier that everything in our personal view of reality is just one experience. If the "I" is the one experiencing, and people tend to report similar characteristics to it, then could it be that the "I" that we experience as individuals is the same "I" that everyone else experiences?

This is an important concept to grasp; let's break it down. Based on what we understand up to now:

- We know we are the observer of our own experiences (there is a personal "I").
- We know we have common experiences with others and that they are also observed (there is an interpersonal "I").
- We know that all there is to the world is experience. Hence there must be an observer of all experiences (there is a universal "I")

It seems unlikely (and counterintuitive) that there would be multiple different forms of awareness. Rather, could there be a universal awareness that is the same in all three cases above? No difference between the awareness of your personal experiences, the shared experiences of others, and the experience of the entire universe?

Cloudless Reality

The same observer is aware of it all. Since we are all a part of the universe, this would intuitively feel right. If so, let's take a moment to contemplate the ramifications of a world consisting of pure awareness.

The universe is everything. All space and all time. Therefore, since we exist, we must be part of the universe. A simple deduction, I know, but important to get straight! It appears then that there are multiple levels to this ubiquitous "I." I cannot see your world, and you cannot see mine. We cannot see what's happening thousands of miles away, but there may be people in that place who can. Also, we can both look at the same chair and have a similar (interpersonal) experience. I'm sure there are alien civilizations light years from here also having experiences. So perhaps all these experiences are part of one universal experience. Hence the universe (everything) is an experience. Since we know experiences happen in the mind, it seems reasonable to deduce that the universe is that mind.

> *The same conscious awareness that experiences our personal thoughts is the consciousness of the entire universe. It is the essence of the universe.*

The universal mind splits itself into individual minds with personal, private awareness. I'm going to call this the universal "I" consciousness going forward but know that I'm referring to the same thing we experience personally when we are aware of being aware. The same conscious awareness that experiences our personal thoughts is the consciousness of the entire universe. It is the essence of the universe. There is no you or me or out there; there is no physical matter. Hang on, what!?

Life in the Whirlpool

No Physical Matter

Bear with me here because this takes time to absorb. An increasingly accepted view on the nature of reality with a solid basis in experience is that there is no physical matter "out there" (we will get into much more detail in Chapter 6). That the world is made entirely of consciousness or awareness itself. That is not to say that objects *have* consciousness since there are no objects out there to possess consciousness. Everything we experience (which is all we can ever know and therefore can be defined as "reality" for us) is one singular experience that we call consciousness. Some of this consciousness is shared across us, some is personal to us, but it is one thing.

Since this alternative view of reality is based purely on our experience, there is no need to postulate an external view of physicality as being made from individual pieces of matter separate from ourselves. Nor do we need to explain the "hard problem of consciousness" (as we explored in Chapter 2) since there is no "matter" out there to construct itself into a brain and give rise to what it feels like to be in love, for example. I'm not saying there are no brains, people, buildings, or stars. All of that is just as true now as it was before you started this chapter. What I'm saying is what we experience is fundamentally mental or mind-based in nature and not physical. Everything else from that point is as valid as it would be in the material view of the world, but as you'll see, there are huge ramifications for how we live our lives.

To recap on the current worldview, which we explored in Chapter 2. Over the past few centuries, the West has been immersed in a physical world called materialism. Objects are made of solid, material things and are perceived "as they really are" by our senses. Thoughts and feelings are complex combinations of electrical impulses the brain generates to keep us alive to reproduce. In effect, we are machines, born into this world with one purpose, to pass our genes on to our offspring, then die. Every experience we accumulate over our lives will end in our death. It is this view that enables the illusory mind to dominate our lives.

If we are part of one universal experience, however, then we are all intimately connected to one another. There is no separation. The objects we perceive, the thoughts we have, and the emotions we feel are all part of something bigger, and as such, those thoughts and feelings contribute to a larger purpose than that of the individual self. Indeed, each person's purpose is intimately tied to an overarching purpose, with each of us playing our part, much like the trillion or so cells in our body. This view is about as far away from a mechanistic and nihilistic view of nature as we can get, yet it's the most intuitive and experiential explanation we have.

The Dreamworld of the Higher Mind

The concept of the world and everything in it being an experience as opposed to a collection of separate objects can be a difficult one to grasp. However, there is a practical comparison to this concept that we can all associate with—dreams. When we fall asleep and dream, we become the dream character (hardly ever someone watching the character you might have noticed). In a dream, you could be climbing Everest or flying to the moon, or maybe just watching TV. The dream feels as real as the "real" world to you at the time. The snow on the mountain, the cold chill of the Himalayan air on your face, the view of the blue Earth outside the window of the spaceship as it hurtles toward the moon, or the clear high-res picture on the 100" TV you're watching in your dream living room. Are any of those things in your dream *actually* real? They are real experiences from the dreamer's perspective—until you wake up and realize it was all "just a dream."

Each of those "real" experiences happened completely in your own mind. One mind, yours, created a whole world as real as the world you perceive in your waking state, with objects, people, thoughts, and emotions as genuine in the moment as the "real world," with a central character experiencing it all. Sound familiar? What if our waking state was the dreaming state of a higher mind? I know it may sound way out there, but why not? The concept is again based on what we all experience, so in that respect has more validity than a dream being a series of neuronic interactions in the brain.

We don't really know why we dream. There are many speculative theories, including expressing unconscious desires and wishes, processing information gathered during the day, and even a form of internal psychotherapy. While we understand that sleep is essential for repairing cells and replenishing energy, dreams have no known direct purpose. Perhaps dreaming, a process of dissociating from our waking mind into a dream character, is simply a part of nature. If that is the case, since we're part of the universe, maybe the same natural process holds for the universe at large. Not to sound too much like the 1999 movie trilogy *The Matrix*[11] (if you haven't seen it, you must!), but perhaps our waking lives are literally a dream of the universe.

> "Brahman, the single unitary consciousness, or absolute awareness, appears as the diversity of the world because of maya or illusion, and hence perception of plurality is an error. The world and all beings or souls in it have no separate existence from Brahman, universal consciousness, and the seemingly independent soul is identical to Brahman."[28]

A world consisting exclusively of purely mental states is called "idealism," the belief that reality is closer to a dream than solid, material stuff "out there." This isn't a new idea. Many Eastern cultures have understood this concept for thousands of years. Indian philosophy, as far back as 788 CE, taught an early version of Idealism through the Vedanta teachings of Brahman:

We'll investigate the spiritual worldview in a later chapter. However, many ancient religious and philosophical masters were teaching this view of the world being more a thought than a thing before science codified the material world.

Whirlpools in the River

One objection concerning this mind-way view of the world is if reality is one singular experience, how can we experience things personal to us and no one else? And why can't we experience things not in our range of perception (i.e., I have no idea what you are thinking right now. I also have no idea what's happening in Alaska)? To explain this, I'll borrow from a modern philosopher who has tremendously affected me and helped guide my understanding of this view of reality. Bernardo Kastrup[12] has authored several books on this subject and uses a powerful metaphor to explain how this could happen. It involves a river in flow, with whirlpools circulating with the currents in the river. Remember, this is only a symbolic way of illustrating what this view of reality and our place is, but it works well.

When a river flows, we often see whirlpools generated from the currents. The whirlpools are not separate from the river, they are made from the same material, but they occupy a seemingly separate space. The river represents universal consciousness, encompassing everything and moving in a certain direction. The whirlpools are representations of localized consciousness, namely conscious beings like humans, dogs, cats, birds, etc., that have formed their own personal conscious experience within the larger stream. The whirlpool forms when we are born (or are conscious) and dissipate when we die when they are "reabsorbed" into the river.

I like this analogy as it's rooted in a feature we see in nature and explains how we can feel separate and yet be fully integrated into reality simultaneously. Being made of the same substance as the river explains how we can share the same experiences yet have a personal world inaccessible to others. We can even use the whirlpool metaphor to explain introspection—effectively, the cyclic motion enables it to see into itself. Barnardo explains in detail his rationale for this model of reality, so I won't go further than this. I've included Bernardo's work in the Bibliography at the end of this book if you'd like to delve into his concept more.

The fact that this is a river and not a calm lake is an important part of this analogy. Rivers are not static, and whirlpools cannot exist in still water. They are in a state of constant motion and have an intended direction. From the waves above to the currents below, it's messy in there! You experience objects passing by you, thoughts emerging, and emotions constantly undulating within you. That is just from your own personal experience. There are over eight billion other human beings on this planet that have their own set of dynamic experiences. How about all the events occurring right now on this planet beyond direct human experience, such as polar bears hunting seals in the Artic or a species yet to be discovered thriving in a thermal vent at the bottom of the deepest ocean? Consider what's happening beyond our planet. Stars are being born and are dying, possibly going supernova. Supermassive black holes are devouring thousands of stars in every one of the two trillion galaxies in the universe. All these things are happening now and have been for as long as you have experienced anything. This constant movement and change are what is meant by the whirlpool analogy above. We are an intimate part of these dynamic experiences within which we possess our own personal experiences and share them with others. It is this combination of experiences that we call life.

Despite the inconceivable dynamism of this river, it seems to flow according to a set of physical rules we have discovered through introspection (e.g., gravity, thermodynamics, hydrodynamics, etc.). This is how we can predict behaviors in our world with increasing accuracy. However, there is a more fundamental, underlying current within the river that drives it in a certain direction. Think of it as the channel within which the river flows. This driving current is the *unfolding of the universe*, and we are in that flow.

> *We are an intimate part of these dynamic experiences within which we possess our own personal experiences and share them with others.*

We can't know the direction of this current explicitly, but we feel it. We feel it as a pull, a deep passion for doing or being something. Every whirlpool has its role to play in the flowing of that river. The closer you can understand, feel, and move with the flow of this undercurrent, the less resistance you will feel to life. That reduction in resistance is felt directly as being more content, peaceful, and tolerant of situations. Overall, being happier with life.

Going with the Flow

The universe is estimated to be approximately 13.8 billion years old, and the Earth is around 4.5 billion years. We can estimate that life of any form started to take hold on Earth after about one billion years, and shortly after that, conscious life started to arise.

The advent of our meta-consciousness (self-reflection) is very recent in the evolutionary timeline of humans. With basic forms of consciousness present some three to four billion years ago, self-reflection only surfaced in humans some sixty thousand years ago. In fact, humans (homo-sapiens) were on the planet and thriving for almost three hundred thousand years before they could introspect. It took an extremely long time, despite the preceding existence of life with even a basic level of consciousness, for introspective consciousness to emerge. We have no idea why it took so long and what caused it to ignite, but we do know that when it appeared, our evolutionary path was exponentially accelerated. Although this ability to "know that we know" something is mostly taken for granted, we have yet to see anything else do this in the universe.

In that respect, then, perhaps the emergence of introspection was part of the unfolding of the universe. Those whirlpools could not only gather information about their surroundings but could now cultivate insights about themselves. All this served to feed the undercurrent of the river to evolve the universal mind.

We intuit that the nature of the universe is to learn about its own nature. Of course, we have no way of knowing this, but we *do* know there must be a rationale for all these happenings. We also know that humans naturally desire to learn more about ourselves and our world, and we are part of the universe. All we're doing in this hypothesis is extrapolating a fundamental human desire to a universal one.

Since the universe is infinite, it cannot entirely learn about itself. It simply can't have an infinite perspective on the infinite. What the universal mind can do, however, is introspect from within, in the same way we introspect from within our minds. This is where the whirlpool analogy works so well. The universal mind (the river) forms local instances of itself (whirlpools) whose agency it can use to "look at itself" from many different perspectives. We are those whirlpools, with our own experiences carried by the current. The current is the unfolding of the universe according to its purpose. The whirlpools are carried according to their own purpose. Your purpose. Take away any of those whirlpools, and the river cannot flow exactly as it should.

> The universal mind (the river) forms local instances of itself (whirlpools) whose agency it can use to "look at itself" from many different perspectives.

To complete the analogy, your purpose is a combination of the universal current and your individual current within that. That combination enables you to freely flow down the river to your destination while experiencing the world for yourself. The secret to living a life aligned with nature is, therefore, to keep your whirlpool healthy and to go with the flow of the river. This itself is analogous to keeping the sky clear of those clouds. If this is true, which maybe it is intuitively felt to be, then our very existence, each of us, is tremendously precious. We each contribute to the flow of the evolving universe. Nothing is separate.

As I mentioned earlier in this chapter, this view of consciousness as the universe's very nature isn't new. It has been the foundation

Cloudless Reality

of many philosophies for thousands of years. Although this view may seem difficult to grasp, as it was for me, I'd urge you to sit back and think about it, perhaps during meditation (see Chapter 8), to see if there's a deeper sense that this worldview could be true for you. Even if you don't get to that point, it is worth having an alternative view of nature to consider, contrasting with the nihilistic view of a purely material and mechanical universe most of us live (and often suffer) in today.

> Take a moment to experience yourself as a whirlpool in the flowing river. This is a popular guided meditation.
>
> Relax and focus inward, then imagine slipping into a gently flowing river. Just float on the river's surface and try to clear your mind. See if you can feel the water's current around you, maybe see rocks in the water as you pass by. You can put your hands in the water to direct yourself around these rocks if you wish, or just gently bump into them. Think about how much effort it would take to go in the opposite direction to the river—how many rocks you might bump into. Does it feel natural to fight the flow?
>
> Spend time just flowing down your river. There may not be an end destination; that's not the point. Just relax and flow.
>
> This exercise is analogous to how we are meant to

> live our lives. Whenever things get too much, I find it comforting to relax and float. It's like a reconnection with where I should be.

I'm sure you've heard people say, "Go with the flow." Now you have a slightly different perspective on what that could mean. Most of the time, you'd hear someone say those words when you experience difficulty or need to make an important decision. Countless stories tell of people who "went with the flow" and found that a solution to their predicament (in the form of objects, thoughts, and emotions) magically appeared for them. Ever wonder how that happens? Whether it's just coincidence, wishful thinking, or something deeper? (Excuse the pun.)

Physical Laws

Another attractive aspect of this mental-only view of reality is that there is no contradiction of the physical laws discovered through the material-only view. Take, for example, the theory of evolution through survival of the fittest. This impressive body of work was presented in Charles Darwin's *On the Origin of Species*,[13] stating that organisms better equipped to survive will grow to reproduce. In contrast, those lacking won't survive to produce offspring. Hence those most suited to their environment are the ones that reproduce most successfully and are most likely to pass on their traits to the next generation. With few exceptions, this theory seemed a reasonable account for the evolution of all species on Earth and was rooted in materialist philosophy.

If the purpose of the universe is to evolve through introspection via conscious beings, then there must be a mechanism to ensure such entities continue to exist. Nothing in this theory is contradicted in the conscious-first model, only the substrate of reality being non-physical. It could also be considered that the vast diversity and obvious creativity we see in the billions of species just on our planet alone gives us some indication that there may be a creative power at work here and not just a random mutation of genes. All the known physical laws, such as gravity, electromagnetism, thermodynamics, relativity, quantum mechanics, and even neuroscience, are conserved under this alternative view of reality.

We've discussed above the premise that the universe has a purpose, to self-realize. We also know that we are intimately part of the universe. So the need to self-realize is also inherent in ourselves. This has been understood and written about for years (see Maslow's Hierarchy of Needs). So, what does self-realization mean to us individually, and how can it be linked to the universal purpose?

Self-Realization and Meaning

Our true nature is that of a silent observer aware of every experience we have. We call it the "I." We also know for sure that there is a voice inside our heads called the Imaginary Me that has been created throughout our lives because of our unique ability to look back on ourselves and form opinions on what we experience there. Introspection is the universe's tool to help it unfold by experience *and* is the source of suffering created by the illusory

Life in the Whirlpool

part of the personal mind. It, therefore, seems that this mind is a necessary part of our purpose in life.

If we are "experience-generators" within the universe, then the Imaginary Me is the source of many of those experiences, both good and bad. Regardless of our experience, this illusion plays a major role in converting what is naturally there to an experience generated through introspection and so "seen" by the universe, enabling it to evolve another step toward self-realization. Therefore, the challenges we experience in life are presented for us (and the universe) to take another evolutionary step.

When referring to "good and bad" experiences, these are, of course, purely human constructs. We have created these concepts so that we can live productive social lives, but they are not a natural part of the world. Most animals have no concept of good or bad, perhaps except for those that live close to humans and so have been taught it. In that respect, the universe is impersonal regarding what happens to us over a lifetime. An experience is an experience, be that the attainment of some kind of nirvana or the death of an infant after birth. Both are required for the universe to evolve. Our "job," then, is to create as few negative and as many positive experiences for ourselves as possible in our time on this planet. We do that not by accumulating things but by aligning our inner world with the outer, keeping our whirlpool clean.

In addition to the experiences created by the illusory self and witnessed by the "I," there is another source of experience we are aware of. Something that every one of us feels deep down. It is an inherent part of the "I" and is again intimately linked to the evolution of the universe. It is essentially the river flow we discussed above, but as experienced in our personal world. Our own purpose.

On Purpose

We all have some intuition of the direction we'd like to go in life. Some people have an affinity to art and music, others to science and mathematics or physical activities such as sports. Often, we have no idea why we have these inclinations or where they came from, but they are powerful enough to direct our lives, be that through careers, hobbies, or lifestyle. When we fulfill the need of this deep desire within us, we feel liberated ("My job doesn't feel like work.") or, as is most often the case, frustrated when they are not realized ("This is not what I want to do with my life!"). These inclinations are the pull of the river of life. The frustrations we experience are like rocks in that river. They prevent us from following the flow and give us a bumpy ride down that river. Those rocks are placed there by us, so they can be removed by us.

Let's break down exactly what's happening here, as we're covering a lot of ground!

1. You are born into the world as a conscious being in a conscious universe to experience it (i.e., itself) through a combination of perceived objects, thoughts, and feelings. The whirlpool is formed.
2. For the first few years of life, the world is viewed by your young consciousness as wonderous, curious, and vivid. This is the rose we discussed. We flow with the river, with no big rocks to disturb us.

Life in the Whirlpool

3. Some experiences arise that don't align with your expectations and create unwanted emotions and thoughts in response. Rather than let those experiences pass, you hold onto them. This is primarily a self-defense mechanism. We hold onto these experiences to be prepared for the next time they happen. We put rocks into the river.
4. However, with your ability to introspect, you extrapolate the initial unwanted feeling to anything remotely connected to similar experiences (the rose thorn and any other flower in our earlier example). We grow those rocks.
5. This process continues throughout your life, constructing an alternative persona within your spectrum of totally false yet extremely addictive experiences. Most people start to believe they are that self, and that initial innocence as a child is lost to a world of fabricated and distorted objects, thoughts, and emotions. At this point, we may lose the natural flow of life and meander aimlessly in discontent. We bump into the rocks.
6. At some point, often ironically around the same time as the Imaginary Me emerges, you find an affinity to something in life. Often this is very clear ("I know I need to be a doctor and help people"). Other times is very vague ("I have this feeling that I need to help others, but I have no idea how"). We feel the current of the river.
7. At some point later (for some people, this happens after they've lived enough life to realize), you feel the river's pull so strongly and the "old" way of living so unfulfilling that you proactively seek the answers to those questions. This is the proverbial

"Is this it?" question that most of us respond to with either, "Probably not, but nothing I can do now" or, "No, and I need to understand what is." We're so over being thrashed by the rocks and feel the pull so strongly we decide to remove them.

It is the strength of the river's pull on us and our ability to manage the illusory voice in our heads that determines what we ultimately will do with our lives and how happy we will be doing it. If the voice is loud, it will drown out our calling with typically critical messages, pulling us further toward the rocks and away from where we are meant to flow. That gap between the river's flow and our internal voice is the source of discontent and incompleteness.

> *That gap between the river's flow and our internal voice is the source of discontent and incompleteness.*

You can't flow seamlessly with the river of life because the voice in your head blocks your way. Hence you either remain stagnant or are thrown from rock to rock as you're pulled downstream. This thrashing represents highly charged emotions and feels uncomfortable. From the perspective of the universe, you'll remember its purpose is to *evolve through self-realization via experience*. In that regard, the universe is experiencing itself regardless of how "happy" you are at any time.

Although the universe seems impersonal from our perspective, I suspect there is some teleological rationale for it calving itself into multiple seemingly separate instances of itself. Considering how long it has taken for beings that could introspect to enter the stage, not to mention the immense suffering that had to take place in that process, it seems a hefty price to pay. Perhaps some of the feelings of incompleteness and disconnection we intuitively feel, often without reason, are due to this seeming separation. Rather like a balloon being compressed, it longs to return to its normal, complete state but must go through the compression many times and from different perspectives before it can be released into the wind. More of the balloon metaphor in Chapter 7.

If you can remove the rocks in the river by reducing your focus on the illusory you—the you that blocks the flow—you can get a clearer picture of your purpose in life and close that gap of disillusionment. You will also more fully appreciate the instrument you play in a universal orchestra. If you weren't here playing your instrument at just the right time, the music would not sound the same. Please remember every note you play (every experience you have) contributes to the piece (the universal song). And, as we'll get into later, your contribution remains well after your physical body ceases to exist.

Our Role and Purpose

I hope this chapter has provided a different way to look at the world, your role in it, and what your purpose means on a larger scale. By considering the basis of reality as mind rather than matter, the foundation for everything we experience is rooted in just that, our experience. We have no need to postulate a physical world outside of our mind that we have no evidence exists. Indeed, by considering our personal and interpersonal experiences a part of a universal experience, the concept of separation is now just an illusion.

I often wonder whether having the ability to introspect serves to cut us off from our fundamental nature. You may be able to conceptualize a model of wholeness, but can you really feel it? Perhaps beings that lack introspection do feel this. A snail cannot self-reflect, but because of this, it may have innate access to the universal mind. We can never know, of course, but it's an interesting thought. If the universe is evolving toward self-realization through us, and we already can self-realize, then we must represent parts of the universe that are also evolving. That makes you, me, and any meta-conscious being a miracle (and an irony) in the universe.

Now you have seen the juxtaposition of the two models of reality and investigated the differences, which view makes the most sense intuitively? I understand it is a big step to move from a material-centric view of the world to a mind-centric one. If this is new to you, it will take time for it to sink in, but when it does, it will change the way you live. In the next chapter, we'll discuss some fundamental assumptions of our current reality. What are the implications of such things as time and free will in a world of mind stuff? Hold on.

Chapter 5

Fundamental Concepts

What Does This Mean for Time, Interconnection, and Free Will?

That sounds like a heavy title! Bear with me. It's well worthwhile investigating some of these most fundamental concepts of reality since they obviously contribute to how we live our lives. How we look at time, how much we feel separate, and the amount of control we feel we have over our lives can make the difference between a life lived in contentment and one in suffering. As we explored our current perspective and the alternative view of reality in previous chapters, you'll find that elements of science, philosophy, and spirituality reinforce some of the previous conclusions. I ask you to consider the material with an open mind. What you'll uncover here are wholly different ways of looking at what you might have thought were mainstays. As we draw back the veil, we'll examine how these different views can positively impact how you think about yourself and others.

Cloudless Reality

What Time Is It, Really?

The first concept, yes, it really is just a concept, is time. Have you ever stopped to think about what time really is? It seems to flow consistently from one moment to the next, with a remembered past and a relatively predictable future. We need time to function as a society, to mark growth, and to contextualize the things we do (making a coffee shouldn't take five days, I'll meet you at 2 p.m., etc.). We see people we love grow from kids to adults, our hair goes grey over time (mine certainly does!), we have memories, and we make plans. All set in an agreed planetary paradigm of 60 seconds, 60 minutes, 24 hours, etc.

In fact, all our experiences (objects, thoughts, and feelings) are rooted in time. When you see a car, you see it now. If it's driving past you, it's gone "in a few seconds." You may think about a loved one after you've spoken on the phone "for a few minutes," and you may feel happy when you have a tasty meal at your favorite restaurant, but that feeling of happiness subsides after you leave the restaurant "a few hours later." Experiences must have a perceived time to understand them and for them to have meaning. When we look at time independent of experience, however, things get a little tricky.

We typically consider time as having an objective quantity (days, hours, minutes, seconds). This is needed when considering "clock time" (hard-boiled eggs take exactly six minutes). However, the concept of clock time is unique to us humans. Does an elephant know what time it is? Do penguins know to only spend 15 minutes underwater? Animals use their natural instincts to

Fundamental Concepts

respond to experiences we see as time-bound. Flowers grow in the summer and die in the winter due to environmental changes, not "because it's been four months." What else is unique to humans? Introspection. The illusory mind. Could it be that our concept of time is intimately linked to those uniquely human qualities?

Although we use objective clock time to function, our time is mostly experienced subjectively. Have you ever noticed a difference in how time "feels" in different situations? An hour waiting for the bus seems a lot longer than an hour watching a gripping movie. If you remember events where time seemed to "stand still', they were probably times of extreme positive and negative emotion.

I recall when I first took a ride on a rollercoaster. I was about twelve years old, in line at Disneyworld for what seemed like hours (probably 20 minutes at most). I remember standing in line, feeling uncomfortably hot in the Florida humidity, looking up at the coaster I was about to board flying past me, with screams of terror and delight in the air. I couldn't wait to get to the front of the line. Eventually, I jumped into the coaster car, full of nervous anticipation, and off we went. I felt like I closed my eyes, screamed, and shouted for a few seconds, then opened them as the coaster returned to the station. Although a fun experience, it seemed to have lasted about 5 seconds. It probably lasted more than 5 minutes. I heard a few kids around me saying, "Was that it?!" I felt the same. "Hours" of waiting for 5 seconds of fun. Didn't seem right. It didn't stop me from going on many other roller coasters that day, though!

How do we know that time is experienced equally by all things?

Cloudless Reality

A leopard may experience a minute in a very different way than, say, a sloth. A female mayfly lives for an average of 5 minutes, the male two days, whereas an ocean quahog (a species of edible clam) can live over five hundred years. How would they experience time if they could, given our concept of time is always in the context of our lifespan? Of course, we can never really know how time is experienced by anything other than ourselves, but that, in essence, makes it more subjective in the way we experience it (and remember, experience is all we have).

Likewise, we claim that the universe is nearly fourteen billion years old, an almost unimaginable number. But is it? By whose scale? If our lives were measured in millennia rather than years, we wouldn't experience it as quite so old. Given the immensity of the universe, it could be that 13.8 billion years is to the universe the equivalent of an hour for us. We simply don't know.

What exactly happened to my sense of time in my coaster experience? Notice that when I was in line, my external circumstances didn't match my internal desires, and time seemed to creep along at a snail's pace. When I had alignment between what I wanted and what was happening (front row on the coaster), time seemed to stop or move at an incredibly fast pace. It seems that our experience of time is dependent upon how our expectations and our experiences are aligned. With full alignment (internal and external experiences completely match), there seems to be no time. The further we get out of that alignment, the slower time seems to get (try extrapolating my waiting in line at Disney to someone waiting to hear if a loved one made it through heart surgery).

Fundamental Concepts

Our subjective experience of time is intimately linked to our alignment with our external circumstances. As we've seen, how that balance is maintained is a measure of how much the illusory mind is in control. In that respect, then, could it be that time is solely used by the illusory mind to assist in its control over us? Our true self, then, has very little need for the experience of time.

> *Our subjective experience of time is intimately linked to our alignment with our external circumstances.*

Reducing Time

It's interesting to see that often when time is included in many scientific theories describing the natural world, it quickly is made obsolete as the complex mathematical equations supporting such theories are reduced. Albert Einstein was famously quoted as saying,

> *"People like us who believe in physics know that the distinction between past, present and future is only a stubbornly persistent illusion."*

Einstein's theory of relativity is the bedrock of our scientific understanding. It can predict natural behavior to an outstanding degree of accuracy. These theories, however, reveal time is relative to an observer's frame of reference. Without going into too much detail on the theories themselves, they conclude that time is not the same everywhere in the universe. The speed of a ticking clock on the Earth's surface, for example, is marginally faster than in

Cloudless Reality

a satellite orbiting the Earth. The difference is very small in that example (about 7 microseconds per day), but the effect is much more profound in higher gravitational fields or for objects traveling close to the speed of light.

There is strong debate today by many notable scientists and philosophers about the fundamental existence of time, with several competing views.[14] This probably indicates that we really don't know what time is!

Given how much of our attention is seated in time, it is certainly worthwhile taking an experiential look at this evasive component of our perception. Let's try an excursion through time to illustrate what I mean here.

> Think about something that happened in the past. It could be an hour ago or many years ago. Ask yourself, did you actually visit that time in the past? Now imagine a future scenario. Again, it can be eating dinner tonight or what your grandkids' weddings will be like several years from now. Doesn't matter. Again, ask yourself, did you actually go to that future point in time to experience those things?
>
> I'm hoping the intuitive answer to both questions was "No." What happened is you recalled a memory from a past event in the present moment, or you imagined a future event in the present moment.

Fundamental Concepts

Since we rely on memories for past experiences and imagination for the future, it could be argued that neither past nor present exist, just our thoughts about them, which are always only happening now. The only element of time that can be considered real is when you experience these thoughts of the past and future. Let's continue with a quick excursion into time.

> Focus on the present moment. The book you're holding, the light in the room, the feeling of the chair beneath you, your breath. Try to stay just in the present moment for about 10 seconds. It should almost feel as though you're falling into the moment.
>
> I know it's not easy to stay anchored in the present. We'll cover much more of that later in the book. For now, just observe what it feels like not to think of the past or future.

Most people live their lives in either of these two realms. That's because the illusory mind needs to stay in your awareness; it disappears in the present, but more of that later too.

Your experience of the present moment is obviously much closer to "now" than thoughts of the past and future. But those experiences you just had of the present moment are no longer in the present moment; they are now in the past, about a minute ago, in fact. If you're thinking of them now, they are again memories

Cloudless Reality

being experienced now. In fact, something you thought of less than one second ago is now in the past, right?

The present moment is like a cloud. As soon as you try to grasp it, you realize you don't really have it. Let's think for a minute (pun intended!) about how long the present moment lasts. Is it a second? Half a second? Seconds are just indiscriminate measurements of clock time created by humans through a combination of the context of their eighty-year lifespan (over 2 billion seconds, by the way) and how much incoming data our brain can process to create a version of reality we can understand in that moment. So, is it reasonable to apply a human measurement on something that happens instantaneously all over the universe at the same "time"?

How about we claim that one "moment" equals 0.0000001 seconds? For us, an unimaginably short period. Our brains couldn't possibly process that small a time increment. Hence that "frame" of reality simply wouldn't exist for us (much like how we can't see the individual frames on a movie screen, we just see a continuous flow of movement). For a much-evolved alien species on a planet hurtling around Proxima Centauri, however, that minuscule increment could represent a lifetime. So if our neighbors there lived an equivalent duration to us, they would also experience 2 billion of their seconds within our 0.0000001 seconds.

So, again, how long does the present moment last? How far do we go? Theoretically, we could reduce this value until it is infinitely small. If you reduce your concept of time to a value for the present moment, you inevitably get to zero.

Fundamental Concepts

Let's think through that again because it's one of life's greatest mysteries. Everything you can recall from your past, and everything you could possibly imagine in the future, as well as whatever you are experiencing right now, is all experienced in this moment, which seems to exist in no time. In the current material view of reality, can something exist in no time? Obviously, then, that begs the question, does time really exist?

*If you reduce your concept of time to a value for the present moment, you inevitably get to **zero**.*

One Present Moment

While you're musing on that one, let's just add that the present moment is the same moment at every point in the universe. That moment may exist at different points in clock time, but there is only one "present moment" everywhere in the universe. So, all reality is being experienced by all of reality in no time. Everything that ever was and ever will be is being experienced now.

As discussed in the previous chapter, we exist as a part of the universe, you are the awareness that observes experiences, and this awareness is the universe itself. So now we can extend this further to say that whatever the universe experiences moment to moment exists in no time. The universe is aware of itself, including its past and future, in the moment but is beyond time.

This is rather like a subjective experience of time when you are your true self. There seems to be no time when we are closer to the "I" of our true selves. So, the natural state of the universe

Cloudless Reality

(including us) exists without time. We only experience time when we are out of alignment with our true selves (the universe). This is when the illusory mind "pulls us" into its illusion of time. Our natural home has no time. You might need to read that a couple more times. I did!

When you fully absorb the implications of this, it's not difficult to conclude that the present moment is the most precious thing you will ever possess, and you possess it, along with the rest of the universe, at every instant. After that instant, it's gone forever. Think, "stop and smell the roses." Most of us spend our lives trying to escape the current moment, remembering some event from the past, or fantasizing about a possible future. That is only the illusory self pulling you back to where it can maintain control. Use clock time to function in society, yes, but let's now put that into context. It's merely a tool.

Okay, let's recap what's just transpired.

The present moment can be reduced to no time.

When there is no time, the illusory mind dissolves.

Therefore, the illusory mind creates the corresponding illusion of time.

When the illusion is gone, what's left is the real you.

The present moment is where you'll find the real you.

Again, we're speaking here of the subjective experience of time. Clock time is a necessary framework for society to function. Ultimately, all time is illusory, but even illusions can be useful! Whenever you hear your illusionary self telling you a story, try to momentarily "break out" and be in the present moment. It can be

Fundamental Concepts

anything in the moment. A view from the window, the feel of your clothes, even just staring at your hand. You'll find that the story you were being told instantly evaporates, just like a cloud(!). Make it a habit to get as close to the present moment as often as you can. Just try to experience the present moment as fully as you can, whenever you can, especially when you wish to be away from the present moment. Those are the most effective times to sink into what *is* right now. This is why grounding in the present moment is a powerful form of meditation. We'll look more closely at that in Chapter 8.

I hope that's provided a different way of thinking about time and the preciousness of the current moment. Now it's time (sorry!) to move on to an investigation of our next fundamental concept. Interconnection.

Interconnected All the Way Down

One of the most common causes of suffering and discontent is a feeling that we're somehow disconnected from each other and the world. That what we do doesn't really matter in the scheme of things. We're insignificant compared to the rest of the universe and can't make a difference unless we're another Martin Luther King or Abraham Lincoln. We often try to take control of situations to address this feeling of inadequacy, leading to more suffering.

In our discussions on the "I" and our unique ability to see ourselves and our contribution to the universal unfolding, I hope you can see that considering yourself a tiny, meaningless fragment is simply an illusion. Despite the reality of our significance, the fact remains that most of us think we *are* individual, separate entities that must be in full control of our situation or that we're lost and scared. Neither of these beliefs is real. Indeed, the opposite is true. We are more interconnected with the rest of the world than we might think. This interconnection is deep and complex, with each connection being as important as any other. Don't take my word for any of that; experience it yourself.

Take a minute to consider what had to happen for you to be reading this book right now? Really sit back and think through the events that led you to be here. You may say that you decided to search for a book on this topic online, ordered it, it was delivered to you, opened it, sat in a chair, and started to read it. Just take some time to break those events down a little more. Just a couple minutes of introspection will do.

Okay, let's break this order of events apart with just a few questions.

1. The book exists because the author (me!) decided to write it. What happened in my life to cause me to write it so you could read it?
Quite possibly over a million things. From a church service on a Sunday when I was six, to a lecture on cosmology at university some thirteen years later, to a random thought on a train in Paris when I was twenty-three. If any one of those things didn't happen

or happened in a slightly different sequence, I may not have written the book you're reading right now, and none of this would be happening in this moment.

2. How did you come to make the decision to read this book?
Many things would have transpired to the point where you Googled for books on this topic. If any one of those things didn't happen to you or happened in a slightly different sequence, you may not have ordered the book you're reading right now, and none of this would be happening in this moment.

3. How about all the people and experiences required to provide internet service to your home so that you could Google the book, read about it, and order it and/or download it?
If any one of those things didn't happen or happened in a slightly different sequence, you couldn't have ordered this book, and none of this would be happening in this moment.

4. How about the delivery of the book to your door?
Probably arrived in a van. Who built the van? Who created the parts that came together to create the van that delivered the book you're reading right now. If any one of those things didn't happen or happened in a slightly different sequence, you wouldn't be reading this book right now, and none of this would be happening in this moment.

Okay, I'll stop there, but you get the point, right? Consider that each one of the dependencies mentioned above will have its own dependencies and so on. Asking just four questions on what seems like quite a simple scenario on the face of it has created possibly billions of interdependencies, just for the present moment you are experiencing to have occurred. That is the case for every moment you and everyone else will have. It's the case for every moment occurring in the universe.

Everything is dependent (or connected) on everything else.

Now, how many dependencies would that be?

The fact is, if you drill into any situation deeply enough, you'll eventually get to an infinite number of dependencies that had to occur for any moment to exist. Another way of saying this is *everything is dependent (or connected) to everything else.*

In the next chapter, we'll take some time to look at how the universe was created from a scientific perspective, but suffice it to say, there was a point in the far past when the universe was one singular thing (called a singularity), that contained everything, yet had no size and existed in no time. From that single point, the universe expanded into the ninety-four billion light-year length it is today (and continues to expand). Back at that singular point, everything was connected to everything else (because everything *was* everything else). We've since learned that expansion didn't break that initial connection. Everything remains connected to everything else. That provides another validation point from an intellectual perspective, but it's more important to experience this for ourselves.

Fundamental Concepts

Let's go back to the book-reading scenario. It's easy to see that you didn't write the book, you didn't decide what would happen that you might want to order such a book, you didn't provide the internet service to your home, you probably don't build delivery vans, you didn't construct the building where you're reading it or the light that you're using to read it. We are more like participants in an internetworked experience that encompasses an infinite number of dependent experiences. This internetworked experience is called life.

The interconnection exercise can be extremely useful when things don't seem to be going "your way," or when you feel somehow separate from everyone else. By taking a step back and thinking through what had to happen for you to be experiencing the present moment, you start to feel less need for things to be different. Each moment you experience is a part of the unfolding of the universe. In that respect, there is a reason why all those millions of dependent events happened in that order and at that time to get you to have this experience. The feeling of being separate and disconnected simply fails the test when considering the interdependencies involved.

When we feel separate, we often feel a corresponding need to try to control situations. If we can control our situation, perhaps we can change it to match what we desire internally, then we'll feel good. This desire for control and the feeling that we are central to a given situation can be very compelling. Are we really in control of anything?

Cloudless Reality

Who's in Charge Here?

Since, as we've seen, there are so many interdependencies for any given moment in time, then what is driving the end-result experience? Who or what is making it happen? Perhaps a more fundamental question is, "What do we mean when we say the *end result experience*?" In the book example above, we anchored the interdependencies to the "end result" of sitting in a room and reading a book. Is that the end of the experience? What events and experiences occur in your life after reading the book? Someone else in your house may pick up the book and read it, too, leading to another chain of follow-on events. We can never say for certain that an event exists at the end of a line of prior causal events, and then it's over. It can never be over. The natural state of the universe is to continuously unfold. It doesn't take a breath. So, if there is never really an endpoint to a situation, who is in control of what? When there are so many dependencies at work for any moment to exist, then it seems intuitive that there can be no central point of authority driving any situation. That means, for the most part, you are never really in control of your life. Most people bristle when I say this, but let's put that statement into context.

The universe is evolving naturally. Much like a flower growing, its petals open out in a way that is totally natural to the flower. The flower doesn't decide how it will grow; it just does. Like the flower, you are also part of the universe, so part of the universal unfolding. Unlike the flower, however, you are aware of yourself through introspection and can make decisions. Although we may feel our decisions are our own, each has its dependencies, most

Fundamental Concepts

of which we don't have cognitive access to. At every moment within the body, myriad mechanisms exist, many far beyond our comprehension. We don't consciously control our breathing, heartbeat, and oxygen absorption into our blood via the lungs' alveoli. We don't purposefully grow older, yet we all do. As we've discussed, almost all the thoughts and feelings we experience are not generated by our conscious volition.

Outside bodies, we may believe we are in control of our lives, our children's lives, or our jobs. For each of these, we can think of countless scenarios, each with countless dependencies not within our control. Say you're a team leader managing ten people. They are essentially under your control and your responsibility. When you ask one of the team to perform a task, you can see how many other things must happen for that task to take place for you to reinforce your sense of control. Since you're not doing the task yourself, there must be myriad other dependencies on the employee. They must accept the task and be able to complete it. They may be unhappy and decide not to do the task, or they may not have the required tools. The list goes on. While there is a sense you are in control, remove any one of those dependencies you have no control over, and you'll find your control diminished.

Although we have little say in how most things happen, we tend to experience this "sense" of overall control. Ultimate control is an illusion. Just another story created to give the impression that we call the shots to make the outside world align with our internal desires. The more these stories of control divert from external reality, the more "out of control" we feel, and therefore more frustrated and anxious. When I say we have "very little control," that's not to say we have no control. In truth, we are more akin to players on a stage. While we have some responsibilities for acting our piece as a certain character, we need the other actors to do their bit—otherwise, the show is a flop. In that regard, we are more like co-creators of each event we experience. We're one dependency in a complex web of interdependencies, but never *the* dependency.

If you can maintain that sense of being a player in the play, then even when you feel you're in control, you are more like an actor playing a role and being directed according to the flow of the performance.

We can play our role, be that of a parent, a manager, or a doctor, and exert the control necessary to contribute to society but remember, we as individuals are not in charge of the whole play. If you can maintain that sense of being a player in the play, then even when you feel you're in control, you are more like an actor playing a role and being directed according to the flow of the performance. When you live like this, the weight of controlling the universe is removed from your shoulders, and you feel more of that interconnection with others. You and the universe are working together to create reality. Much like a river and whirlpool!

The Actor's Free Will

If we are not wholly in charge, what does that mean for free will? I would argue that free will, as we collectively tend to understand it, doesn't exist. Now that's not to say that we're simply automatons with zero control over our destinies. Still, the impetus that drives any experience we think we initiate (from buying a house to picking up a pen) is, as we've seen, not just the result of an independent decision to do it in that instant.

Consider the simple act of making a cup of coffee. To initiate the experience, "you" decide you want an espresso. Where did that desire come from? When did you first start to enjoy espresso? Maybe a friend introduced you to them on vacation in NYC. The internal signals in your body that tell you that you want coffee maybe arise from a need for caffeine. That's a series of chemical reactions in the body sending a message to the brain for more caffeine, nothing to do with your free will (unless you are consciously manufacturing hormones inside yourself!). Again, I'm not saying we don't have any free will, but we need to put it into perspective. As we've investigated, the control we believe we have in any situation is only a small part of a tapestry of interactions and dependencies that result in an action that, on the surface, looks like it was wholly initiated and executed by us. However, an almost infinite number of things had to happen first and at the right time and will continue afterward.

Our sense of free will is also an act of co-creation between the unfolding of the universe and an intention we create as a player on a stage. The actor can say a line in the play in a manner that they believe best represents the character and the situation they find themselves in at that point, but only at that time and in that context. In doing so, they will influence the play's action, but they

Cloudless Reality

won't be controlling it. Since they are assuming a character, in the moment, they aren't aware that they are saying a line in a script. To the character on stage, it is their decision to say the line at the right time. In that sense, it *feels* like their own free will. Same for everyone else.

The combination of the script, the direction, the lighting, the sound, and, yes, the player (you) saying the right lines at the right time, but *in the way you decide to do it*, creates a Broadway hit.

Our sense of free will is also an act of co-creation between the unfolding of the universe and an intention we create as a player on a stage

Our sense of free will is an important aspect of our lives, without which we would just be manikins, spouting our lines without meaning, with an audience lining up to leave. If we were to understand that this is not a one-person play, that there is a cast of literally billions of other players playing their parts, we would remove a huge burden from ourselves.

Tying It All Up

From a simple investigation into your experiences and a pinch of common sense, you can see that time is, at best, a tenuous concept. In the present moment, the universe is experiencing memories of past events and any possible contemplation of the future. That's the very definition of the infinite. Yet we've experienced that the present moment doesn't exist in time. If the present moment is timeless and infinite, containing everything we can experience,

Fundamental Concepts

then that must be where we truly exist. We're not material machines in a time-bound universe. Rather we're immersed in the mystery of "everything in nothing." The illusory self pulls us out of the timeless mystery and imprisons us in a time-bound fight to survive. Grounding yourself as close as possible to the present moment will reward you a thousandfold in closing the gap between the real and the illusory you.

Most of us believe we are separate from each other and the world, where what we do in our limited time has little impact. As social beings, our natural state seeks connection to others (why is solitary confinement used as a punishment for the incarcerated?). So, when we feel disconnected, we have corresponding feelings of incompleteness and unease. Since, as we've seen, every one of our experiences depends on every other experience, nothing could be further from the truth. Separation is just another illusion—albeit a compelling one. If we all truly believed and experienced this interconnectedness, how could we feel lonely, separate, and disconnected? Likewise, how could we collectively experience jealousy, greed, and violence? Have you ever felt overwhelmed when a random person smiled at you while walking down the street? Why is that? Maybe it's because, at a deeper level, we already know our nature is connectedness, that we are all basically the same threads coming together to weave the tapestry of reality. Humans long for this connection to others because our natural state of connection to everything is masked by the illusory self we've built. Know that when you look into another's eyes, you are intimately connected to them. Especially when you experience negativity with someone else. Know that you are connected at a fundamental level. Look for this connection in your life, and you'll find those sparks of wonder start to appear more frequently.

Knowing that you are part of an interconnected world means your actions create causality down the chain that could affect millions of other positive and negative events. We are not a separate and individual piece of the universe devoid of any real significance or impact and longing for connection. Our actions can have a monumental impact in ways we will never know. A smile at a checkout clerk, the right text at the right time, stubbing your toe, buying fruit at the local market, who knows! Nothing is pointless. Everything matters.

We are not the center of and in total control of any situation. When we believe that, we take on the pressures of that responsibility. As we've seen, the responsibility for any situation is a combination primarily of the universe unfolding and, secondarily, your introspection at that point in time. When we take on the responsibility for all of it, we feel unbearable pressure. Much like muscles giving way to a weight they were never built to hold, we then get stressed, burned out, and exhibit any number of other dysfunctions. This false scenario is the cause of most of the mental health symptoms we present.

When you feel a genuine sense of interdependence and your part in the play, the weight is removed, as are the resulting emotions. You may find that your actions in this context are far more effective than those taken under the stress of exclusive responsibility. That shouldn't surprise you since you share responsibility with the

Fundamental Concepts

most powerful force imaginable. Everything is teamwork.

Take the pressure off yourself to take control of every situation and consider your actions simply part of the natural unfolding of life. When you think how many experiences must conspire to bring the current situation in front of you, it reduces the pressure to take things so seriously. Yes, we have some say in what happens to us and the world, but for the most part, our job is to step back and let nature unfold as it does. We can do this by first fixing our internal state. We'll talk more about how you can do exactly in a later chapter.

Time, Connection, and Control

We've spent some time in this chapter diving into the nature of time, connection, and of control, and free will. Since these are major drivers of our sense of self, I hope you can see how simple concepts have been contorted and cause us to feel discontented. The need to be away from the present moment, the feeling of separation, the desire to be in control, and the assumption of exclusive free will, are all driven by the illusory mind. As you explore how to live life with this phantom, remember what you get back in your life in doing that. All the reasons why life seems inadequate, that you're missing the point in life, all that is addressed when you clear those rocks from the river, go with the flow, and take your role in the universal play. Nothing could be more important. Except for my mixed metaphors!

Many of the points presented here are supported by science today, and almost all have been taught in spiritual and philosophical traditions. It's almost as if we are waking up to what the sages of the East have been saying for over three thousand years. We could even be approaching a point of reconvergence between scientific discovery and spiritual teaching.

In the next chapter, we'll get into more detail as to what science tells us about the true nature of reality based on what we see and how this correlates closely with what people have intuitively known to be the truth through the ages. This is where I get my quantum mechanical and relativity groove on. Let's go!

Chapter 6

The Universe Inside

Are Science and Spirituality the Same Thing?

Since I was very young, I've loved TV shows about science. Space, planets, black holes, the universe, you name it. It may seem obvious to most, but it struck me in my early teens as I watched one of these shows that the narrator kept referring to the universe as a thing separate from us. The universe consists of stars, galaxies, and planets "out there" that we can observe from "here." The narrator also said that "the universe" was everything that exists in space and time. So I concluded that as well as being "out there," the universe was also "right here." The Earth was part of the universe. England was also part of the universe. My town, my house, my room, the floor, the furniture—all part of the universe. I concluded that "*I am part of the universe.*" My senses are part of the universe, every cell in my body is part of the universe, and even my thoughts and feelings then are part of the universe, and obviously, so is everyone else's.

Cloudless Reality

The Universe Inside

When you hear someone say, "The universe is inside you," that is literally correct. On clear nights I try to remember to look up at the sky momentarily and know that we are part of all that. That makes me feel very small and very special at the same time.

My fascination with the vastness of the universe and wanting to understand why we're here and our role in it led me to pick up a book many years ago called *The Tao of Physics*, written in 1975 by physicist Fritjof Capra.[15] In it, he draws striking comparisons between modern physics and Eastern spiritual traditions such as Buddhism, Hinduism, and Taoism. I'd never been into Eastern teachings before and primarily read the book to get a high-level overview of spirituality in the language of science.

Although I didn't recognize it as such at the time, I was a staunch materialist. It was atoms all the way down for me. Spirituality wasn't grounded in what I understood from empirical evidence. This book changed my opinion on all that permanently. I remember sitting in Chicago O'Hare airport waiting for my return flight back to NYC (I spent a lot of time sitting gate-side in those days) and flipping through the pages of this book, engrossed. I knew a decent amount about the scientific breakthrough discoveries and gradually learned some of the fundamentals of these far-distant spiritual teachings. As I turned page after page, it became clear that what these sages were saying—including Jesus, Buddha, Lao Tzu, and many other enlightened beings through the centuries—drew almost the same conclusions as quantum mechanics, relativity, and wave theory today.

Moreover, they connected the impersonal investigations of science to the very personal experience of spirit. In retrospect, I can see now why that shouldn't be a surprise. Science seeks to understand the nature of the universe, and that is what we are. It seems logical then that an investigation into the nature of the cosmos, from atoms to galaxies, is also an investigation into the nature of ourselves. Spirituality seeks the same things, only from a different perspective.

> *Jesus, Buddha, Lao Tzu, and many other enlightened beings through the centuries drew almost the same conclusions as quantum mechanics, relativity, and wave theory today.*

Seeing this close relationship between the external world of science and the internal world of spirit led me to several insights into what we're doing here. Hence, it's useful to look at some scientific topics and compare them to the teachings of a few historic spiritual masters. Perhaps you can see what I saw there too.

Universal Moments

Over 13.8 billion years, the universe has evolved from the big bang, essentially a single point devoid of space and time (since time didn't exist before it), to something of an inconceivable size, containing all things and all time. There are approximately a hundred billion stars in our Milky Way galaxy and about two trillion galaxies in the known universe. Earth is one of eight planets circling an average star in an average galaxy. The nearest star to our sun is Proxima Centauri, 40,208,000,000,000km away.

Cloudless Reality

Do the math. The universe is vast. I mean really vast. We are small potatoes in the scheme of things, but we *are* a part of it. We may be small, but as far as we know, we're the only known instance of the universe being able to make the statements above about itself.

Consider all the things that had to happen in the universe's evolution for us to exist to experience it? Gases coalesce to form stars that, after billions of years, explode, releasing many elements that make us human beings and all other living species—carbon, iron, calcium, phosphorus, and many others (yes, it's true to say we are made of stardust). Remnants of dead stars formed planets that, over billions more years, cooled down and, if the combination of elements were just right, evolved basic life. Countless more millennia and *conscious* life emerged, eventually evolving to attain introspection through human beings (and almost definitely other alien species in the universe).

Given this vastness, how many "moments" do you think are taking place at every point in the universe right now? I'm sure there isn't a number we can conceive of to show that. An almost infinite amount, certainly. How many experiences are taking place on Earth at any given time? Still a number with an incalculable number of zeroes after it. Since the universe, by its very nature, is constantly unfolding, then these "moments" also pass by constantly. Now consider how many of those moments *you* are experiencing right now? One. Of all the myriad things taking place in the universe at this very moment, we only ever experience one of them.

So why do we put so much importance on the moment unfolding before us?

The Greater Landscape

Every moment you experience is one infinitesimally small part of a greater landscape of moments occurring as the universe unfolds. In that respect, the moment in front of you is no more or less important than any other moment. Yet we give it primary importance because it's ours.

Imagine if you could be as impartial about the moment in front of you, regardless of what it brings, as you are for the myriad moments you're not experiencing. That's not to say we don't react appropriately to the moment, but we contextualize it, reducing its ability to impact our emotional state. We already know that the reason why we don't like a particular experience is because it's not in line with our internal expectations. When you take a moment to consider all the things you're not experiencing, it helps put your "special" moment into context.

Of all the myriad things taking place in the universe at this very moment, we only ever experience one of them.

I have a poster of a photo called "The Pale Blue Dot." Pictured below, it's a photograph of Earth taken on February 14, 1990, by NASA's Voyager 1 space probe from about 3.7 billion miles away.[16] Looking closely, you can see Earth as a tiny dot among bands of sunlight reflected by the camera toward the center of the image. *Voyager 1* was leaving the Solar System and turned its camera around to take one last photo of Earth.

You can see photos on NASA's website here: https://solarsystem.nasa.gov/resources/536/voyager-1s-pale-blue-dot/

Cloudless Reality

I look at this photo often. It's a stark reminder of our place in the cosmos. All the worries, anxieties, expectations, and realizations of every human being occurred on a speck of dust, on the outskirts of a spiral galaxy, one of two trillion. I don't mean to belittle our beautiful planet, but in the scheme of things, consider how important missing that meeting is compared to our place in the vastness of the universe. When I was busy taking flights around the US for my job, I often looked out the window as the plane flew over a populated area. Looking down on the houses of hundreds of thousands of people and thinking about their lives, their experiences, their problems, and their worries. I found this contextual reset soothing when the molehills of life are made mountains by the illusory me.

Thinking about the vastness of the universe and the millions of individual lives prompted more questions about reality. When I combined what I knew of the strange world of quantum mechanics with what I knew of the spiritual traditions, it was almost like a spiritual awakening. Let me explain.

The Quantum Enigma

Ever heard of quantum mechanics? This scientific theory of the subatomic world is the most accurate representation of our observations of reality today. Sparing you the details on what can be a complex subject, I want to share the results of a very interesting experiment that first took place in 1801 by British physicist Thomas Young, called the "double slit experiment."[17] In my search for observable, experiential evidence of the link between science and spirituality, this experiment was instrumental for me, especially since it has been re-created thousands of times, producing verifiable results. There is some science here but stay with me, as the conclusion of this experiment is core to our journey.

Young's rationale for his experiment was to understand a scientific conundrum that existed at the time regarding light. Although light has always exhibited wave-like properties (e.g., refraction, diffraction, interference patterns), other experiments had shown light clearly exhibiting solid particle-like properties (called photons). Obviously, light couldn't possibly be both a particle and a wave, so more investigation was needed.

Young fired a beam of light toward two vertical slits in a board and recorded where the light ended up on the other side of the slits using a photographic plate. If light was particulate in nature, then the pattern expected to be shown on the photographic plate would be two discrete lines, where each photon of light had individually passed through one of the slits and been detected. However, the experiment's results showed a ripple-like interference pattern on the plate, clearly demonstrating that whatever had passed through the slits was a wave and not a discrete object. (See the diagram below). Young, therefore, concluded that photons clearly exhibited wave-like properties.

Experiments conducted to verify the particle nature of light continued to show high repeatability, so the "wave-particle duality" mystery remained. Intrigued, Young tried to identify the property of light more accurately by firing just one photon at a time at both

Cloudless Reality

slits. Surprisingly, the wave-like interference pattern still appeared on the plate. A single photon split in two, passed through both slits and interfered with itself to create the interference pattern like a wave. Clearly, an impossibility if the photon is a discrete object.

To observe what was happening specifically at each of the slits as the photons passed through, detectors were placed at the slits, and photons were again individually fired. When the detectors were activated, the pattern on the photographic plate showed two single lines aligned with the slits. The same pattern would be expected if the photons were discrete particles. When the detectors were switched off, the pattern returned to the wave-like interference pattern.

Despite a seeming impossibility, the results clearly showed that the properties of the light depended on the detectors being on or off at the slits (i.e., whether the photos were being observed). The light behaved like a wave when not observed, then changed to a specific object in space (a photon) when it was observed. This experiment has been repeated many times with several types of detectors, even using electrons and other elementary particles, with the same results.

There was only one conclusion that could be drawn. At the sub-atomic level, the detection of solid objects (particles) is wholly dependent on them being observed. If nothing is present to observe the particle, it reverts to a wave with no defined spatial location. Since these waves can extend in every direction infinitely, they can contain an infinite number of outcomes upon observation. We simply don't know where a particle is until we decide to look

The Universe Inside

Young's double-slit experiment

at it. Since the universe is assumed to be made entirely from these elementary particles, it would seem, from scientific inquiry, that everything we experience is only made real for us by observing it.

What do we mean when we say "observation"? Since the photon could only be detected as an object when the detectors at each slit were switched on but reverted to waves when switched off, observation cannot be the presence of an inanimate object. It was only when the scientists viewed the output from the detectors that the nature of the light changed. Hence, when we say "observation" in this case, it could be more accurately defined as "conscious observation." It seems reality can only manifest by including a conscious observer—by consciousness itself.

> *It seems reality can only manifest by including a conscious observer—by consciousness itself.*

Cloudless Reality

Infinite Possibilities

With no conscious observer, the universe is an indiscrete field of infinite possibilities. Since we are conscious observers, we are integral to the manifestation of the universe. If you are intrigued by the implications of Young's Experiment, I urge you to dig deeper into it. There are subsequent insights that have been gleaned from this experiment that are even more mind-blowing, including implications to time and free will, but too detailed to cover in this book.

The double slit experiment was one of the first observable and repeatable examples of the strange nature of quantum mechanics (QM). QM is a fundamental theory in science that describes the physical properties of nature at the scale of subatomic particles. It has proved to be a highly accurate method for predicting the behavior of natural systems. It is utilized in many essential technologies we take for granted today, such as GPS, MRI scanners, and solar cells. In essence, QM indicates that we can never know the exact location of a sub-atomic particle until it is measured through observation. At this microscopic level, reality is only "real" when observed. Upon observation, the "probability wave function" of an object collapses to a definite location in space and time—the wave is made material. So, we have a theory of nature that states that nothing is real until it is observed, and this theory highly correlates with what we see in nature. There are other implications of QM, such as entanglement, that also demonstrate high levels of interconnectedness across the universe.

There seems little doubt today, over 220 years since Young's experiment, that QM is showing us a view of reality validated by observation. Hence, the very act of being aware of reality seems to bring that reality into existence. Awareness, or consciousness, seems to be a major component of our reality. Perhaps science is close to concluding it is all there is to our reality.

As Physicist Max Planck, founder of quantum theory, stated back in 1931:

> "I regard consciousness as fundamental. I regard matter as a derivative of consciousness. We cannot get behind consciousness. Everything that we talk about, everything that we regard as existing, postulates consciousness."[18]

If you think back to the discussion on the awareness of your experience being the foundation of yourself and the universe in Chapter 3, there seems to be a clear correlation between QM's "quantum field of probability" and this field of awareness. You might conclude that all the objects, thoughts, and emotions you experience only exist in your perception (and therefore exist to us all) because they are observed by universal awareness. In essence, the same "I" that is aware of your feeling of sadness is the same "I" that is aware of a photon of light passing through a slit in a board in 1801.

If you're in the science camp, you could say that reality is a universal quantum field of infinite probability, being reduced by conscious observation into a localized physical or mental object of experience. Since the quantum field has infinite possibilities, at any point in time, an infinite number of outcomes are possible depending on observation. Awareness creates reality. Got it? Okay, let's move on from the science of the very small to that of the very large.

It's All Relative: e=mc2

For centuries, the prevailing scientific doctrine accurately describing and predicting the macro-world we experience, like footballs, planets, apples from trees, etc., was Isaac Newton's theory on gravity around 1666. His mathematical formulations of the interactions between large bodies are still used today to predict planetary orbits and to get astronauts to the moon. Indeed, Newton's various scientific theorems are still taught in schools today. The predictable power of these theories, however, began to fracture as we evolved technologies to look way beyond our planet and began to see anomalies around massive objects such as stars and distances that required considerations close to the speed of light.

In 1905, Albert Einstein formulated his theories of relativity and, without going into too much detail here, reformulated Newton's model of bodies being attracted to each other through an unforeseen force called gravity to a model that explains this supposed attraction through the curvature of spacetime by massive objects, much like how a bowling ball distorts a trampoline when place in the middle. Einstein was a mathematical genius, no doubt, and the equations he used to derive his theorems were so complex it was thought only a handful of people could understand them during his lifetime. One of the most famous of his equations is known for its simplicity, albeit derived from some highly complex mathematics. You may have heard of it:

$$e=mc^2$$

This beautifully simple yet massively impactful equation states that energy and mass, or matter, are essentially the same thing: e=m. The value c is the speed of light, which is a huge number at 186,000 miles per second. Since c is a constant, the equation simply says that energy and matter are equivalent, but given the size of c, there is a huge amount of energy for any given amount of matter. Indeed, this equivalence powers the sun and every other star in the universe. We could say our very existence depends on matter and energy being equivalent. This equivalence has since been used in many practical applications, from nuclear power stations to car engines to mp3 players. Unfortunately, it was instrumental in the design and successful use of the atomic bomb, much to Einstein's despair.

Note the omission of any dependency on time in the equation. Einstein initially factored time into his earlier formulations, but as he progressed through what must have been a herculean task of deriving his equations, he quickly found that the value of time was not required to arrive at the simplest, and therefore most natural, formulation. Hence, energy is the same as matter without regard for the passage of time.

> *We could say our very existence depends on matter and energy being equivalent*

We've known for hundreds of years that energy is effectively a field of vibration, and a field is a wave. This wave can vibrate at different frequencies, correlating to different energies. This is how we can microwave our food and get sunburned on the beach. Not

Cloudless Reality

the other way around!

Given the conclusion to the slit experiment we explored earlier, it makes sense that, some hundred years after Young, we were able to scientifically prove that:

matter = energy = a field of vibration

It has been a well-established law of physics[19] and experimentally verified by Émilie du Châtelet in 1722 that energy is conserved throughout the universe. That is, there is a fixed amount of energy throughout the cosmos. It can be changed into different forms (fields, matter, etc..). It can be moved around and merged but never destroyed. We cannot create more of it, either.

Now consider the "types" of energy you know exist from your direct experience. Electricity is energy, magnetism is energy, heat is energy, and when you move your arm, that movement expends energy. Anything else? How about a little respite from the science, and we have an experience together?

Close your eyes and spend a minute or so stilling your mind and body.

Think about your body. See if you can feel an energy, a vibration inside. Move your arm in front of you, then put it back. Did you feel that you used energy to do that? Don't think about moving your arm. Just feel the energy inside you being used to make the movement happen.

Now take a minute to bring up an emotion. It will

probably be related to thought and can be happy or not (probably not too emotional either way!).

When you sense an emotion surfacing, *feel* where it is in your body. Sometimes people feel emotions in their stomach, chest, or solar plexus. Wherever you sense this emotional charge, really focus your attention on it. Feel as though you are falling into the feeling. Remove all thoughts associated with it. Just experience the raw emotion.

During this exercise, you may have felt tangible energy being tapped inside to enable the physical movement of your arm. By going deeply into a singular emotion in the body, you may have felt a strong, energetic charge associated with it. When you really focus on any emotion to the extent that you can remove the thoughts associated with it, it starts to simply feel like energy inside you. Neither good nor bad, just a raw, energetic vibration. The movement of your body and the act of thinking and feeling are all a flow of energy inside you. Much like how the wind is felt, it isn't real in itself, but rather the movement of air molecules resulting in pressure differentials you can feel.

We learned from Einstein that matter, including your body, is equivalent to a vibrational energy field. From your experience, you can likely see that so too, are your movements, thoughts, and emotions. You could therefore conclude that your physical body, the thoughts you think and feelings you feel, are, in reality, a field of energy. This field can vibrate at different frequencies, with each vibration experienced as something specific, such as a particular thought or emotion. The only difference between your hand and your feeling of sadness is its vibrational frequency. Since energy is conserved, then the energy that you are can never be destroyed. It can be changed, moved, or merged with other energies, but its nature is infinite.

Since all we know of the world can be categorized as either matter (atoms, our bodies, our planet, the sun, etc.) or fields of energy (electricity, magnetism, gravity, thoughts, feelings, etc.), then we can extend the model of our experience being a field of energy to the universe being the same thing. Again, we are the universe, so this intuitively makes sense. Using only logical extension to the scientific mass-energy equivalence, we could state that the universe is one energy field. Much like the river has waves and ripples, with every ripple being an intimate part of the river, the universe is chaotic with vibrational energy. We perceive it as objects, thoughts, and feelings, but at its basic level, it's a field of vibrational energy. Overlaying this field with quantum mechanics brings us to the conclusion that this field of energy is probabilistic in nature. It is merely in "probable" form until it is observed by consciousness. And the same is true of the universe; until it looks at itself.

So, to conclude, you, me, our thoughts, feelings, and every object we can perceive exist as a field of energy with a probability of existence. When that field is consciously observed, the reality is made real. In this respect, reality feels increasingly more like a dream than a solid, physical system.

Bringing It All Together

Having examined some ground-breaking scientific discoveries, let's examine where they align with our discussion regarding a consciousness-centric view of the world, interconnectedness, and time.

We looked at the big bang theory of the universal genesis, where everything in existence in this moment emerged from a singularity. Since the universe contains all space and time, then before the existence of this singularity, there was no space and time. Hence the creation point of everything was not in time and space. If you recall our discussions on time earlier in the book, we concluded through our personal experience that the present moment contains everything from the past and future, including the now, yet exists in no time. Essentially the present moment is "everything in nothing." The same description we use to refer to the big bang. I'll leave it to you to continue to walk that cosmological path if you so wish!

Since everything emerged from this singularity, at some point, everything was connected to everything else. As you look at the interdependencies in your everyday actions (like the

Essentially the present moment is "everything in nothing." The same description we use to refer to the big bang.

"reading a book" example in Chapter 3), you may start to see the strong correlation between your personal experience of interconnection and the birth of the universe.

Progressing to the strange world of quantum mechanics, Young's experiment demonstrates what we have traditionally come to understand as objects (namely complex combinations of atoms and sub-atomic particles) behave more like waves of probability and are only perceived as solid objects when a conscious observer is aware of them. Hence consciousness must be present for anything to exist in our reality. Since, in addition, this quantum field has infinite possibilities, then at any point in time, an infinite number of outcomes are possible depending on observation. The wave-particle duality demonstrated in the double-slit experiment provides scientific evidence that parallels an experiential worldview of interconnection and co-creation. We, as conscious agents, not only experience this world but actively contribute to its manifestation—its unfolding.

The infinite number of possible outcomes for our reality could explain the mind-blowing diversity of the world, not only on our planet but in the observable universe. We discover species on this one planet that we couldn't even imagine before observation (I've always wondered why the platypus is the way it is!). Science fiction is regularly trumped by the reality of cosmological observation.

We, as conscious agents, not only experience this world but actively contribute to its manifestation—its unfolding.

Finally, we spent some time with Einstein's famous equation $e=mc^2$ where we discussed the implications of the equivalence of matter and energy. We concluded that we, along with everything else in the universe, are a field of vibrational energy. One field, infinitely interconnected, infinitely probabilistic.

Thanks to the genius of such scientists as Einstein, Born, Heisenberg, Pauli, and countless others, we have peered into the nature of reality from a purely analytical perspective and found a fundamental correlation between those theories and our experience. Combining these correlations provides a compelling case for a world that, rather than consisting of separate objects, is more a single field of possibility. One where consciousness is not only required for it to be experienced but is the foundation of it all.

Religious and Spiritual Correlations

There are many other examples of these scientific and spiritual correlations, far too many to include in one chapter of a book. However, we would be remiss to omit some notable spiritual pioneers and see how their teachings correspond to the scientific and philosophical discoveries we've discussed. Let's review what religion and spirituality say about this worldview and how they correlate to science and philosophy.

I understand religious interpretations can be subjective and intensely personal, so forgive me in advance if I come to conclusions that you would not. I only ask that you consider the below in your context and see if you have the same experience.

Christianity

I'm by no means a deeply religious person, but attending a church school as a child exposed me to many of the teachings of Christianity. As I've read pieces of the Old and New Testaments over the years, I've understood more and more of what was being said back then. I believe that much of what was being communicated in those texts was more symbolic than literal, and I've interpreted such texts in that manner. Let's take a few examples from the bible and see if we can link them back to all we've learned thus far.

The Adam and Eve Story in Genesis

To begin, Adam and Eve lived in full peace, innocence, and bliss in the Garden of Eden, being at one with God and in fascination with everything. They had no preferences. Everything from food to shelter was taken care of for them. They didn't need clothes, so they roamed naked. Eventually, they were tempted by the snake to eat from the Tree of Knowledge. They both ate the fruit and immediately felt ashamed of their nakedness. Adam even tried to hide himself from God. The peace and wonder of the Garden were now obscured.

I hope you can see a correlation with the "Rose and Thorn" story from Chapter 2. Initially, Adam and Eve are like young children, where the world is just one big adventure to be discovered. We don't worry about being naked, nor are we concerned about what other people think of us. As we mature, however, we inadvertently eat the fruit, symbolizing the temptation to seek, crave and resist the material world. It is at this point that we can see ourselves (our nakedness in this case) and begin to feel negatively about it. It is the symbolic birth of introspection. The

> *Our lives are meant to be lived as a balance between our true selves and the self-knowledge of introspection. The illusory self is meant to be here.*

tree of knowledge is where the illusory mind is created, and once the fruit is eaten, the true nature of God (the wonder of the Garden, the observing "I', the universe in pure form) is obscured, rather like clouds obscuring the blue sky.

Note also that the tree and the fruit are part of Eden. God placed the tree in the Garden. The Garden would not be the same without that tree. Our lives are meant to be lived as a balance between our true selves and the self-knowledge of introspection. The illusory self is meant to be here.

The Prodigal Son

The parable of the prodigal son represents God's unconditional love for us as His children. Even if we leave Him, even if we sin, even though we are demanding and can lose our faith, He still has faith in us. Eventually, the prodigal son returns and is welcomed.

Perhaps the departure of the prodigal son represents the universe needing to calve itself into multiple seemingly separate instances of itself, so those instances can view the universe from which they came and therefore evolve. As we've said, experiences are what the universe needs to evolve. It doesn't matter what those experiences are (sins, demands, faithlessness); each is valuable learning. However, the universal mind yearns for completeness and gladly welcomes back each separate part of itself when it returns:

"Man shall not live by bread alone, but by every word that proceeds from the mouth of God."

Matthew 4:4

Cloudless Reality

You will not find your purpose by relying on the material world with its cravings and resisting. The "mouth of God" is the "I", and knowing who you truly are is the only way to relieve your suffering:

> "I am the Way, the Truth, and the Life. No one comes to the Father except through me."
>
> John 14:6

As God's son on Earth, Jesus was a human being that had reached the point where he truly understood how to live a life free of suffering, discontent, and disillusionment. By paying attention to all the messages he was giving, you could create your own path to liberation from suffering (come to the Father). In effect, use him as an example. He is human, and if he can do it, so can you. There really is no other way.

> "Do not be anxious about tomorrow, for tomorrow will be anxious for itself. Let the day's own trouble be sufficient for the day."
>
> Matthew 6:34

Live in the moment; it's all we ever have. The present moment is infinite and is the doorway to freedom. So don't live in the past or future; live now:

> "For God so loved the World that he gave his only Son, that whoever believes in him should not perish but have eternal life."
>
> John 3:16

The Universe Inside

Akin to the universe divesting itself of unity, to calve itself into multiple seemingly separate instances of itself so that those instances can view the place from which they came. This is a massive price to pay for the universe, but it is the only way it can evolve. We have this constant feeling of incompleteness because we are truly incomplete. We are obscured from the source so that that same source can experience itself. We are collectively the "sons of the universe." If you understand that we are here to gather experiences and then return, you are free from disillusionment (have eternal life).

> *"All my authority in heaven and on earth has been given to me."*
>
> Matthew 28:18

"He" is all of us. We all have the authority. Notice he says all MY authority is given to ME. It's always been His (ours). We are not trying to regain something; it has always been here, albeit shrouded. We just have to remember it.

Buddhism

Let's look at the teachings of one more notable spiritual sage known to all of us. Siddhartha Gautama, later known as Buddha (c. 563–483 BCE), taught his understanding of the world through the Four Noble Truths:

- Life is suffering.
- The cause of suffering is preferences (attachment to external things)

Cloudless Reality

- The end of suffering comes with an end to these preferences.
- There is a path that leads one away from craving and suffering.

Taking the Four Noble Truths and recasting them in the context of what we've been discussing in the book:

1. **Life is suffering**: It's important to accept that a key part of the human experience is suffering. Buddha didn't mean physical pain. That's a natural response to a problem with the body. The suffering is psychological. The often-unnecessary pain we experience due to seeking and resisting experiences. Rather than conveying a negative perspective, suffering in the Buddhist view is more of a pragmatic view of the world. It's unavoidable and necessary, but it can get out of control when we give the wheel to the illusory mind.
2. **The cause of suffering**: This is the voice inside our heads that constantly needs to seek or resist the world (over which, as we have seen, it has almost zero control). This voice is the Imaginary Me, self-created over years of resistance to external events.
3. **The end of suffering**: This comes with an end to this seeking and resisting things so the real you can shine through. We may never end suffering completely, but we can all reduce it significantly. Certainly, enough so we can more clearly sense our purpose in life.
4. **The path away from suffering**: There is a way to overcome this suffering. Although Buddha created a beautiful pathway in the Noble Eightfold Path, the most direct way to achieve this

is simple. If you refuse to let your preferences dictate your life, you clear the way for your true self to shine.

As one of the largest spiritual teachings in the world, with over 400 million followers, Buddhism is perhaps most closely linked to scientific thought. It should be no surprise that there is an obvious close correlation between science and philosophy here.

Hinduism

Indra's Net, or Indra's Pearls, is a well-known metaphor used in Hindu teachings at around 1000 BCE and later spread into Buddhist traditions, symbolizing the universe as an infinite web, every node of which is both an individual entity and inseparable from the whole. This net is spread in all directions, and at each node of the net sits a reflective jewel (or pearl). Each jewel reflects every other jewel; hence no single jewel exists independently but is a part of the whole. One jewel missing means the net is incomplete.

The correlation here is surprisingly stark, given the age of this story. Rather than a collection of independent entities, the world is an interconnected whole, with each part dependent on every other part. Each "node" of the net contains the whole net within itself. The metaphor points to the belief that we are nodes in this net. That without each one of us, the net is incomplete. That we see all others as reflections of ourselves and of everything else. That the entire universe is inside each of us. Consider Indra's Net as analogous to the universal quantum field, where everything is interconnected and, like an ocean, every part contains the whole.

Cloudless Reality

The similarities, given the three millennia difference, are quite astounding.

The Common Thread

Having taken a journey through some of the most impactful scientific theories and spiritual teachings and combining those with the experiential explorations in the prior chapters, I'm hopeful that you can start to see there is a common thread running through them all. That our human essence is one of completeness, interconnectedness, peace, and happiness (after all, isn't that what we all desire?). This essence is infinite in possibility and is not bound by time. Every single experience contributes to a universal unfolding that our human mind cannot comprehend. That a necessary part of human nature is self-realization, but with this gift comes the challenge of an illusory self.

It is the unchecked cravings of this illusory mind, the gap between our lives and our innate purpose, together with the constant desire for the universe to return to wholeness, that creates our feelings of discontent, disconnection, and unease. Truly knowing and experiencing this and being able to live in the world with this knowledge is the key to being free of those negative feelings and living a life aligned with your purpose.

So, having taken a journey through some old and new realities and experienced the potential we all possess to move beyond our current predicament, let's look at how we can achieve this.

Chapter 7

We ARE Awareness

What Do We DO With All This?

Having laid the foundation of how the world really is, looked at our role in it, and delved into validation of this view through introspection, science, and spirituality, let's spend some time answering the question, "What do I do next?" In this chapter, we'll get much more tactical on clearing the river of those rocks so you can experience the flow of life. When that happens, you enter a new world of possibility and perspective. I remember reaching this point. Where this different way of looking at the world was fixed within me. It happened gradually at first, by dwelling on some aspects and doubting others. There were other periods of almost explosive revelation where I thought, "How could I not have seen this? It's obvious!" I hope you experience that sensation too. You know when you are aligning with your purpose in life, when you feel the resistance to what is start to dissipate. This is literally you aligning with the universe, and remember, you *are* the universe. When you get in alignment, then the real fun starts.

Cloudless Reality

Aligning with Purpose

If you don't yet feel this alignment, this change in your perspective, don't worry. As you look at your experiences in the world through a slightly different lens going forward, you'll notice your perception may have changed. It took me a few years and many books, meditation, retreats, and podcasts before I was ready. For others it can happen just walking down the street. We will likely experience a radical change in perspective in the moments before death when it's too late to affect change. However this alignment comes about for you, trust that its timing is also part of the unfolding of the universe. You will intuitively know when the time is right.

This different perspective seems intuitive to many, as its basis is in personal experience and not in what we've been told to believe without experiential proof. This is the most foundational aspect of making tangible changes and, as such, is important to recognize as we move into the process of waking up to real life. We talked about this at the start of the book and referred to it many times throughout, but I'll reiterate it here, given its importance. The only thing we, and anyone else, can ever know for sure is that we experience things. We are aware that we are aware of our experience. There is nothing else for us that can be verified as real.

Given this as fact, then the only thing we can say for sure that we know exists is awareness itself. Without awareness, we wouldn't be aware of anything, including that we are aware! Hence awareness is the ground state of reality. Awareness is who we are when everything else we cannot verify as real is stripped away, including our perceptions, thoughts, and emotions.

We ARE Awareness

When we live from the awareness perspective, we live our "default" lives, our true lives. The lives we were always meant to live. What does a "true life" look like? Well, what is that one thing that everyone strives for? A great job, a loving relationship, a nice house, a fast car, world domination? Or even the cessation of negative experiences, such as ending my pain, getting out of this toxic relationship, and finally quitting this job.

If you think about what these bring you, you can boil it down to one word.

Happiness.

In fact, if you think about anything you desire and trace it back to its root, you will always come back to happiness. Try it yourself. There are no genuine desires in life that take you to sadness, anxiety, or anger. These aren't desires in themselves but rather simply a lack of happiness. Even the illusory self acts from its own distorted view of happiness. Its frantic attempts to change the external world to match its internal desires, although ultimately resulting in suffering, are rooted in a deep desire to be happy.

The only thing we, and anyone else, can ever know for sure is that we experience things. We are aware that we are aware of our experience. There is nothing else for us that can be verified as real.

Given that, let's use an analogy to illustrate the tension between happiness and what we believe brings us happiness. It's this tension that causes feelings of emptiness. It's also the pathway to liberation from that emptiness and onto our true path.

Cloudless Reality

Balloons in the Cloudless Sky

Earlier in the book, I used the analogy of an inflated balloon to represent the natural state of the universe, and since we are part of the universe, this is a great way of looking at ourselves. Let me explain.

When a balloon is inflated and sealed, it exists in its true nature. A balloon has been designed to be inflated, not a deflated piece of rubber. An inflated balloon is stable, light, and has a purpose, to float off into the sky. This is akin to us in our natural, *happy* state. In that state, we are balanced, stable, secure, and aligned with what we are here to do. However, we tend to push in on this balloon, trying to make it an unnatural shape. Think about pushing in on an inflated balloon and what that means.

Most of us are oblivious to what we are doing, but in our seeking happiness, we do the exact thing we shouldn't do. We try to mold ourselves into something we think we should be (the pressure on the balloon) instead of just letting it be (a balloon).

First, you're trying to mold the balloon into something it shouldn't be, hence the resistance you experience. Secondly, you expend a huge amount of energy trying to change the balloon until, eventually, you decide it's not worth it, or you run out of energy. Either way, that balloon will return to its natural state one way or another. It's just its nature.

So why do we press on the balloon? Since the inflated balloon without any force on it represents the natural state of the universe, it also represents our true state. Most of the time, however, we can't see that true image of ourselves because it's masked by the Illusory mind. Since we can't see the full picture, we poke and press the balloon to discover its shape. Most of us are oblivious to what we are doing, but in our seeking happiness, we do the exact thing we shouldn't do. We try to mold ourselves into something we think we should be (the pressure on the balloon) instead of just letting it be (a balloon).

So, what is pressing down on this balloon?

Resisting What Is

Any experience rooted in seeking something or resisting something is to achieve happiness. The great job, the loving relationship, the nice house, the fast car, world domination, an end to my pain, getting out of this toxic relationship, and finally quitting this job. Trying to "find" our life's purpose can also be a distortion. A major source of our discontentment in life is caused by the resistance to the natural state of the balloon.

It's important here to distinguish between the events in our lives and our resistance to those events. The pressure on the balloon isn't created by the events. They are what they are— just part of the universal unfolding and, as such, are totally natural. What is unnatural and creates pressure is our *resistance* to the events happening. We cannot reduce the pressure by changing external situations so they are "nice." That is impossible (as I hope you've seen). Reducing the pressure is achieved by accepting life's situations and managing your reactions to them so they don't distort you.

Cloudless Reality

If we all crave happiness in some form, then expending huge amounts of energy to deform the balloon into something that is *not* happiness seems strange and futile. Our challenge is to see we are doing this and stop. However, our efforts to deform the balloon into a shape we believe it "should be" has become our lives. Since most of us are unaware of the balloon, what we feel is a frustrating, continuous resistance to what we're doing, even though we earnestly believe we are doing the right thing. That continuous resistance is felt within us as discontent and unease. You feel incomplete deep down because when that balloon is deformed, you aren't complete.

Continuous resistance is felt within us as discontent and unease. You feel incomplete deep down because when that balloon is deformed, you aren't complete.

There will also be times when there is more extreme pressure on the balloon, for example, when a relationship ends. *"That wasn't supposed to happen! I've failed myself."* Feelings of sadness, anxiety, guilt, regret, and maybe anger arise within. Imagine these as major pressure points on the balloon. Your reaction to the circumstances you experience results in a deeper-than-usual depression on the balloon, causing it to deform more severely. The deformation takes you even further away from your "happy" default state and expends a lot of energy in the process (ever feel drained when you're going through a difficult situation?). Between these bouts of extreme pressure, most people experience constant light pressure on the surface. Sometimes subtle, sometimes a little more pronounced, but always some sense of resistance.

How do we know the pressure is there? Until we experience our true selves, where nothing internal or external can bother us, and when we can just be the independent observer of our experiences, the balloon will have some force against it. If we could only see what we are doing to ourselves this way. If you can see what the balloon is and what is pushing down on it, then perhaps you'll also see the futility of this way of living and try to keep our balloon as close to "normal" as possible.

Before we move on to talk about practical steps to take to reduce the resistance in our lives, I'd like to hold the balloon analogy for one more thought. Consider what can happen when you've reduced the pressure on the balloon. Actively reducing this pressure will almost immediately create a sensation of relief and reduce our feelings of incompleteness, but this is just the tip of the iceberg. When that balloon is as close to its natural state as possible, it can follow the wind and float away to where it needs to go. Stay with me here. I know we're stretching the balloon analogy a little!

Since the balloon is a metaphor for your true state, when you take your hands off the balloon and remove the deformities, your true state moves according to its intended purpose. Not only have you reduced negative feelings, but you also cleared the way to see more clearly what you are here to do. If you juxtapose the image of someone desperately pushing down on a fully inflated balloon versus watching that balloon soar into the sky, as balloons are naturally inclined to do, what image feels more attractive? When

Cloudless Reality

we accept "life is what it is," we find lightness and freedom, so let's go flying.

It Is What It Is

Humanity has existed so briefly compared to the universe that we might as well round that as a percentage to zero. We are literally a blink of an eye in universal terms. Yet we tend to believe that the current moment should be how *we* want it to be. We are in a constant struggle to maintain a balance between the universal moment and our personal desires. Who do you think would win that fight?

We've talked about how, through the awesome complexity and interdependency of the world, the current moment we are experiencing (which we know is the only real moment) is just a step in this evolutionary expansion. We've mentioned that to the universe there are no good or bad experiences. Everything is an experience that contributes to its own evolution. Looking back at our discourse on free will, anything we experience is an act of co-creation, with the universe as the primary creator. Except for a small amount of free will, the current moment you are experiencing is, for the most part, nothing to do with you. The following excursion helps to make sense of this.

Imagine walking through the woods. The sun is shining, the birds are singing, and you are listening to music on your phone. You feel relaxed, open, and receptive to the natural world. Look around you at the trees, the flowers, the blue sky, the bright sun, and the birds soaring high above the treetops. Listen to the gentle rhythm of the music through your earphones. What a great decision you made to come here. Stay here as long as you wish. It sounds nice!

Nothing you saw in your woodland experience was of your creation. You obviously didn't create trees or flowers or birds. The sun has been shining as it is for over 4.6 billion years. Even the music you were listening to was built by countless others, as were the shoes and sunglasses you wore. You may have experienced happiness or be flooded with thoughts of the last time you went on a woodland walk like this. Many of those thoughts and feelings were not created by you. They arose themselves with little personal advocacy. The decision to come on the walk may seem like it was completely your decision, but what experiences did you have before making that choice that may have influenced that? Perhaps experiences that you weren't even aware of.

This is a great exercise in humility. I use it as often as I can in situations around me. Especially difficult ones. The truth is, we play, at best, a marginal role in creating any moment we experience. Things mostly just happen in our field of perception, both internal (thoughts and feelings) and external (objects and situations), and we react to them.

The reason why I shared this experience with you is this. The more you consider the present moment honestly, the more you realize that the universe, which we are a part, is doing its thing whether we like it or not. We cannot change how trees grow, birds fly, or your phone is made. The external world as it presents itself to us *is as it is*. It's our resistance to this basic fact of life that causes us problems. Let me illustrate with a couple of more familiar examples.

You can't find matching socks when you're running late for work.
"That's not fair!"
"How could this be happening today of all days?"
"This always happens to me."

The coffee from your local barista isn't as strong as usual.
"They don't care."
"I come here every day; you'd think
they'd take more care of me!"
"I need strong coffee. This is ruining my day."

Honestly, you can probably think of a hundred more similar examples, maybe even from today! So can I. The fact is that that sock IS missing, or that weak coffee IS weak. They are what they are. It took billions of years and an incomprehensible number of dependent events to happen for you to be experiencing that particular event. You can either choose to dwell on the apparent unfairness of it or think that that is just the universe doing its thing right here, right now. You can then choose to act or just let go. The key here is letting go.

Letting Go

As we've said, most of our experiences are just that, experiences. They move past our field of perception and away. However, some experiences don't make it past our perception. We hold onto them, some for a long, long time. Ironically, the experiences that we hold on to are often ones we didn't want to have to happen or that we crave happening again.

To rephrase this, we tend to hold onto external experiences that don't conform to how we want them to make us feel inside. Holding onto these experiences often results in their acquiring a life of their own, impacting and creating many other thoughts and feelings way beyond the original reaction. This is the exaggeration of emotions we've talked about prior.

Let's look at the "weak coffee" example above. Rather than accept that "it is what it is" and let go of the feelings of disappointment and frustration in that moment, what if you held onto them? What if you think about that weak coffee every time you take a sip? What if you have a disagreement at work that day and blame it on not being fully caffeinated? What if you unreasonably blame the barista for the weak coffee and refuse to speak to them next time? It may even provoke those same feelings of frustration whenever you drive past a coffee shop.

The key here is **letting go.**

It sounds ridiculous, but consider your reactions to trivial encounters, and you'll find something similar. It's how we are wired. The same could be said for very positive experiences we don't wish to let go of. We want to relive them, but most often, the attempt to recreate a prior experience is a far cry from the original (looking at an impactful piece of art the first time is never the same on the second look).

For reasons that will become clear, I vividly remember being sold a car, I think it was a Ford, by a guy named Tommy when I was eighteen years old. That car was a total mess, costing me hundreds of dollars I didn't have to keep on the road. I felt cheated and angry. I didn't let that feeling pass. I held onto that unwanted experience for a long time. Many years later, I still bristle at the mere mention of the name Tommy, or Thomas, or Tom. It's not a pleasant feeling and is consequently one that I try to avoid if I can (if a guy comes to fix my roof and he says his name is Tom, I will instinctively keep a closer eye on him than if he was a Paul. Completely unreasonable behavior!). I don't think I've bought a Ford car since too.

Holding onto emotionally charged experiences contributes to the Imaginary Me. To use the balloon analogy, consider these trapped experiences as pressure points on our balloon. Again, to be very clear, I'm not saying the experience causes pressure, but holding onto and exaggerating our reaction to it does. As we accumulate many of these trapped experiences, we start to create a complex map of "the world how it's supposed to be" inside of us. We spend most of our lives trying to make the outside world match our illusory world inside by avoiding as many of these trapped experiences as possible. The accumulation of these experiences that we've tried to avoid, or tried to repeat, creates the Imaginary Me and is the real source of our disillusionment and unease.

We ARE Awareness

We can free ourselves of the pressure points on the balloon and, piece by piece, dismantle the illusion by following a simple process laid down by others through millennia. As we work through these trapped energies, we release the pressure on our balloon and see a clearer picture of our true selves. Trust me when I say this is key to finding more peace and contentment.

External events will rise to challenge us; that is the universe's very nature. Navigating these challenges without obscuring our true selves is why we're here. It is the definition of human life.

It's important to understand, in clearing away these trapped experiences, that their natural state (as is everything in nature) is to be free. They should not be in there. They should have been released as soon as they were experienced, just like when we experience traffic lights and trees. We pushed them down there, and only we can let them go.

The Process

The process of releasing this pressure is suspiciously simple, but it does require effort. Whenever you feel resistance building, coming from a desire for things outside to be acceptable inside, you "enter the moment" and try to take a step back from the reaction. I find that immediately relaxing the body in that instant helps me. It's difficult to be tense and reactive when you're relaxed. Giving yourself a second to consider what is happening can often be enough to pull you out of getting caught up in the drama. Think about the things we discussed in the book and maybe use them as a checklist to reset your context. Try it now.

The checklist for letting go is as follows:

- This is the universe unfolding as it should; nothing to do with you.
- We are all interconnected, so you are a part of this experience. It's not happening "to you." Remember, how you respond to this right now will impact beyond anything you can imagine.
- If the reaction involves another person, you know you are part of the same "I." In the truest sense, you are engaging with yourself.
- The present moment is the most precious thing that exists in the universe. It's the only thing! Do you want to waste it on a bad experience?
- There are an infinite number of things going on in the universe right now; why are you so concerned about this one?
- Now that you know you will store this inside of you, do you really want to do that?

Know that when you pause, you can decide your next move. Either keep it and let it wind you up, or let it go. If you want to be free, then you literally drop the reaction. Picture holding a microphone in your hand, lifting it before you, relaxing your entire body, and dropping it.

It's that simple. Physically relax your body, and drop the feelings, thoughts, the reaction completely. Then, and only then, can you decide to accept it or do something about it.

What we're doing here is the reverse of what caused the emotion to be trapped in the first place. Rather than suppressing it, squeezing it down, we open it up. Imagine the emotion as a coiled spring being unraveled as you let it go. We don't force it to leave. There's no pushing or pulling here. In fact, there's no effort at all.

I understand that stepping through the checklist in the sub-second timeframe you have to break the flow in a present-moment situation seems difficult, but trust me, after doing this a few times, you'll run through that list instantly. From my personal experience, I know that if you discipline yourself to do this, any action you take afterward will be real and, therefore, will come from a more peaceful place. Releasing the reaction lets it go, which is what it is supposed to do, and prevents it from being stored inside to cause more angst later. It's also one less piece to contribute to the destructive illusory self.

I'm not saying walk away from any situation, by the way. If the coffee is weak and you'd like to have a stronger Joe, then ask for one, but now you'll do it from a place of neutrality. The way you ask the barista and the way they respond will be quite different than if you'd allowed yourself to be pulled down into a reactive experience. Eventually, you'll get to a place where walking out of the coffee shop after having been served a weak coffee will feel the same as experiencing a cloud passing overhead. It just does what it's supposed to, and you let it be. I'm also guessing the replacement coffee will be ten times better than any coffee you've had from that barista before. That's what happens when you start to align with your true self. Happiness shines through, in this case, in the form of a magnificent espresso!

Although the process of "letting go" seems simple, it does require attention and patience. It isn't easy to first identify when you need to intervene and to go through the process of letting go when emotions are riding high. This is like exercising a muscle. The more you do it, the easier it will get. Start with simple situations with low emotional charge (like ordering coffee) and graduate to more intense ones as you work through it. You mustn't be too hard on yourself for failing to recognize or not being able to interject. This is all very new to most of us. You are literally interrupting a temporal flow that has been in place since you were about five years old, and that will take time to master, but willpower is a strong adversary. Use it.

Wearing Down the Rocks

We've talked about how to deal with situations in the moment that have the potential to contribute to the Imaginary Me and enable the feelings of discontent and disillusionment to continue, but how about existing trapped experiences? Those rocks in the river need to be worn down and eventually removed so you can get into the flow of your life. Letting go of prior trapped experiences is similar to releasing emotions you experience in the moment, but there are a couple of differences.

Looking back at the discussion on time in Chapter 5, you know that past and future don't exist, rather are only memories of the past and projections into the future that are experienced in the present moment. In looking at thoughts and emotions created in the past, it's important to remember that the only thing we experience in those trapped feelings is a reaction to the memory of that experience right now. The event itself, no matter how traumatic it may have been, no longer exists. As you look to reduce the impact of previously stored experiences, remembering this fact certainly removes its power.

The fact that these are prior trapped experiences means they may have been there for some time. These trapped energies can lay dormant for years until triggered, and they can also be strengthened when they're given any attention. So, there will be many of these emotions that have been there and possibly have been growing for years. In that respect, they typically can't be removed in one go. There will be a process of wearing down the energies until they become moderate enough to try to remove. Ensure you've practiced releasing the experiences that trigger smaller emotions before you graduate onto the more challenging ones.

Since previously stored emotions typically don't appear in your perception in the moment as present-moment reactions do, you can never be certain when a prior-stored experience will be triggered and surface to your awareness. Sometimes we are aware of triggers and try to avoid them, but often we have no warning, and an old friend could raise its head totally unannounced. Again, this is simply the act of nature unfolding. In that respect, its appearance at that time is perfect. It's happening for a reason that is far beyond understanding. However, since nature's innate tendency is to move toward its realization, then these arisings should always be considered in your favor, even though most of the time it may not feel like it. Have you ever heard the adage "the universe only gives you what you can handle"? Well, this is maybe what that saying was referring to. Trust that each time you experience a highly charged emotional event, whether in the moment or a triggered emotional response to a stored experience in memory, you know it's happening for a reason. If you couldn't handle it, you wouldn't have it there. So, when a trigger from a trapped emotion arises, follow the same process as you would for a present-moment reaction. Use the checklist. Do this each time the same trigger experience arises, and you will soon start to feel less energy created each time it comes to the surface.

If you feel brave, you might want to *proactively* release experiences from the past. Again, I strongly suggest starting with low-emotion experiences and building from there. Jumping into significant life trauma could inadvertently trigger a reaction you don't need. There is a reason why you've suppressed more significant experiences; they are not pleasant experiences, and so the deeper they are, typically the more emotional charge they have. Since these are the larger rocks in the river, wearing them down and eventually removing them releases a significant part of the river, and you will notice the change in flow.

The Sedona Method

Another method of proactively identifying and letting go of past experiences, thoughts, and emotions is The Sedona Method,[20] created by Lester Levinson and passed from Lester to Hale Dwoskin forty years ago. Feel free to visit the Sedona Method website to discover more about this process, but I'll summarize it here.

The method is similar to the process of letting go, except this time, you purposefully choose either a past memory or a feeling that you want to release from your body. You could choose to let go of feelings of inadequacy due to imposter syndrome in a new job, or maybe feelings and thoughts of lack of money or lack of a relationship. You may have experienced a recent event that you can't let go of, for example, receiving an email from your boss that hints that you may be losing your job.

> *Rather than suppressing these thoughts and feelings and giving them more power to affect your state of mind later, move through a process of relaxing the body and releasing the feelings associated with these events.*

Rather than suppressing these thoughts and feelings and giving them more power to affect your state of mind later, move through a process of relaxing the body and releasing the feelings associated with these events. Although it will feel counterintuitive, the most effective way is to bring up the triggered and stored emotion. Try it now:

To use the Sedona Method, use the following steps:

1. Bring up the emotion that arises when you recall the event and focus on that feeling. Not the thought or the memory of the event. Those are stored appropriately as memories. The emotion is trapped and wants to escape, not the memory.
2. Feel the emotional charge. It will probably feel very strange and uncomfortable but stay with it. You may even feel the energy associated with it. That's good.
3. Now the most counterintuitive part of this technique is to welcome the feeling. Smile and imagine welcoming it with open arms. Give it space to be and almost feel like you're one with it. This action starts to unravel the stored emotion and gives it room to dissipate. To release it, you're doing the exact opposite of what locked it down there in the first place.
4. Having spent a few seconds in this welcoming feeling, release the emotion as we discussed earlier. Drop it. Let it go. You may feel the emotion evaporate from you. Some people often have a very physical sensation in this releasing process.
5. Now see how you feel about that same emotion. It may not have disappeared completely, but often it will feel lighter.

You may have to use the Sedona Method regularly, depending on how much energy is associated with the trapped emotion. Still, I assure you from my own experience each time you complete this releasing process, you can feel the energy reduction. That's a sure sign you're whittling down that rock.

Making Progress

Whether spiritual or not, making "letting go" a part of your life is a spiritual journey. You are doing the internal work to clear the way for your true nature to shine. You then feel more alive and aligned with your purpose than you ever can be.

If you're not spiritual, look at this as a healthy way to live from a purely psychological perspective. Isn't this what most mental health treatments are geared towards, the removal or at least understanding of unwanted past trauma? Either way, try this for a few weeks to experience the truth yourself. You can then make your own mind up as to whether it works for you.

An important skill required for all these exercises is mindfulness. It's difficult to interrupt a present-moment event if your mind is distracted. It's even more challenging to get your head into the right place to surface past experiences and feelings to let them go. Although we will get into more detail on this in the next chapter, practicing mindfulness meditation is beneficial in exercising the releasing muscle. I always think of meditation as the gym workout and the process of letting go in the moment, the main event. More to come on this. But how do you know the letting go process is working?

Cloudless Reality

You will know when a trapped experience or emotion has been successfully released in two ways. First, whatever experience created a historical trigger is lodged in memory, and since it had a strong emotional component, it will quite possibly stay in memory forever. There is nothing wrong with that. In fact, it is a necessary use of your memory to learn from it rather than dwell on it. The fact that you'll be able to recall this memory of your own volition and have no strong emotional response to it is a sure sign you've made progress. Second, since that stored experience has now been fully expressed through letting it go, it doesn't need to surface to your perception. You may retain a distant memory but seldom think about it or be triggered by it. That's real progress. Another piece of the sky has just become clearer for you.

By working hard to proactively interrupt present-moment awareness of possible triggered situations, you'll eventually run through the checklist and let go intuitively. It just becomes part of how you interact with the world. I'm not saying that every situation you experience going forward can be instantly released. Still, you'll find that you will look back at events that previously triggered a strong response and will barely even remember experiencing them.

For any strong emotional triggers you experience, you'll have a much higher probability of detecting them, even if you cannot let them go in the moment. I typically make a mental note of these throughout the day (yes, there are often several per day!) and run through a releasing list at the end of the day to "tidy up" those loose emotions, lest they get pushed down and stored.

If you work these practices whenever you can and consider the alternative view of the world as presented in this book, you'll start to feel ease and happiness appearing throughout your life. These changes may be subtle at first. I started to feel much more engaged when listening to people (a challenge for me in the past), often feeling that I was beginning to listen to people with my whole body, not just my ears and eyes. I also began to feel people connect with me when I was talking in a way that seemed somehow deeper, more connected.

You will probably have people you know notice changes in you too. Your mental and physical health and sleep will improve, as will your relationships with others and your work. You may find a streak of creativity starting to show itself. Nothing here is miraculous. If your sky has been heavily obscured for a long time by those clouds, you may not have seen much of the true you shining behind them. So, in that respect, anything could happen as these clouds dissipate! One thing is certain. Whatever comes through will be much closer to the genuine you and, as such, will be accompanied by those long-elusive feelings of happiness and contentment.

Since you are clearing away trapped emotions to enable your true self to shine, it shouldn't be surprising that your external experiences begin to align with your true self too. One of the most recognizable situations you will experience as you practice this cleansing is finding that things start to "go your way" more often. Let's explore this a little since there has been some debate about what this means.

Cloudless Reality

Going Your Way

By "go your way," I'm not talking of a Law of Attraction at work. A much-misunderstood concept, the Law of Attraction is based on asking the universe for something you don't already have but desire. This is akin to wanting the outside world to match your inner world's desires. We have discussed at length how this isn't how the world works. Those internal desires have been created by all those unwanted prior experiences hiding out there and are based on an illusion.

Since we know we desire happiness at our root, putting an "order" into the universe for more money or a relationship is the same as asking the universe to make you happy by aligning the external world to an illusion. You already are happiness! That is your natural state, the blue sky, the inflated balloon. So why ask the universe (of which you are a part) for something you already are? That can never work, and the universe knows it!

However, when you begin to align your internal state to what the universe is already doing outside, not only do you start to feel the happiness of your true self, but you can align with the infinite potential field of the universe. So, you can't help but co-create situations and experiences that enable you to feel your innate happiness. Since this universal field is infinitely probabilistic, anything can happen when you're aligned. I'm sure we've all experienced instances where we experience something completely unexpected, miraculous even. It wasn't. It was just nature doing its thing.

When you start feeling the happiness that arises from the

alignment of your inside with the outside, the desire for those material objects you used to believe brought you happiness simply doesn't have the same attraction they used to. Life itself becomes much more about living it than getting through it.

Don't be surprised when you feel happier about getting a delicious cup of coffee from your smiling barista than you would be getting a Lamborghini on your driveway. That's the real Law of Attraction (rather "law of alignment") at work.

Beginning the Purpose Journey

As you start to feel resistance release, you'll also experience internal and external things that are signposts to your life's purpose. They may be subtle at first, or they may come like a thunderbolt. Rest assured that the reason for you being on this planet at this time will start to shine through the space you've created by removing those rocks.

You may be reading this book because you've already been feeling a pull to something else in your life. Maybe not quite defined yet, but undeniably present. This is the light of your true self trying to shine through the illusory self you've created. It's not hard to see that as you wear away that illusory self, more of that light will shine through. Since everyone's purpose is unique, I can't tell you exactly how your purpose journey will go for you, but I can share what it was like for me so you can maybe understand how this works.

As I shared in Chapter 1, I probably began this journey when I was a child, with an avid curiosity for science and pondering on the big questions. Even though I ultimately decided to pursue a business career, this raging curiosity never left me. In fact, it grew stronger. Maybe like you, as the years passed, I felt tangibly the pressure of the balloon to be more myself. I didn't know exactly what that was, but I knew it was grounded in all the subject matter I've put down into words in this book. As I learned about the illusory mind, I began working on my inner state feeling less resistance and more clarity in my life. It became increasingly obvious that I needed to get this message out. If you'd asked me a year ago if I could write a book on this passion of mine, I'd have laughed you out of the room. Yet here you are, reading it!

Along the way, several serendipitous events cleared the way for me. When these first happened, I was in awe. When they happen now, I am hugely grateful for them, but I am no longer surprised. Why should I be? When we're in alignment, the infinite field of universal potential converges (in science-speak, the wave function collapses into the real) to co-create situations and things that push you on your way. You will find this too. Be observant and watch for harmonious experiences. They may be very small, almost unnoticeable, but they are there. Some will inevitably be mind-blowing. Not only will they help you progress, but they will also be a sign that you are doing the right thing.

Remember that progressing along your line of purpose is an act of co-creation between your role in the universal unfolding and your actions as a self-aware part of the universe. That means that as you clear your view and start to feel the pull of your purpose grow in strength, the willpower and ability to self-realize that you have as a conscious being can be put to their intended use.

You were given these unique abilities to do your part in aligning with and realizing your purpose via experiences for the universe. So, for example, let's say you're the CEO of a company with a burning desire to improve leadership. That pull will be made very clear as you start to clear the blockages of the illusory mind. You may experience spontaneous opportunities to move in that direction (invited to give a talk on leadership at your local school, maybe). As you follow this pull, not surprisingly, you will feel happier and more content and see more things happen to guide you in the right way. Now this is a human life.

Your part in this flow is to observe these experiences and use them to make decisions on what you will do next. I've recognized even the smallest of coincidences in ways I never would have in the past. Since all events are interconnected, anything that passes my way that seems coincidental or synchronous in some way with my purpose, I make a point to acknowledge it. I may not do anything, but it's important to acknowledge the moment. It's an experience, after all.

The act of *co-creation* is an important point to make here. Don't make the mistake of thinking that realization of your purpose is riding the river downstream listlessly. Letting go is an important part of this process (you don't try to swim upstream), but you do have hands in that water that can subtly direct you downstream. The universe will let you know if you're interfering too much; trust me!

As you progress in the direction of your purpose, don't

Cloudless Reality

lose focus on the act of letting go of any unwanted incoming experience. The fact that you are experiencing clarity, reducing resistance and unease, and feeling more happiness come into your life, doesn't mean that the external world will always magically align with you. It doesn't (and shouldn't) work that way. Even the most enlightened beings to walk the earth have cautioned that the act of observation is an ongoing one. As Jesus said:

> "Be dressed ready for service and keep your lamps burning, like men waiting for their master to return from a wedding banquet, so that when he comes and knocks, they can immediately open the door for him. It will be good for those servants whose master finds them watching when he comes."
>
> Luke 12: 35–59

Remember our discussion on time in Chapter 5? Be aware as you progress through the purpose journey that there is no timeline associated with it. Few people arrive at a definite point saying, "I did it. I'm awake now! I see my purpose." It is a gradual process akin to your merging or unfolding with the rest of the universe. Since this moment doesn't exist in time, and all things past, present, and future all exist in this moment, you are already fully realized and awake to your purpose right now. You just haven't experienced it yet. If you are

If you are vigilant of your inner state and help co-create whatever you're being drawn to do, things will unfold as they unfold.

vigilant of your inner state and help co-create whatever you're being drawn to do, things will unfold as they unfold. Letting go of the temptation to either speed things up or doubt they will happen is just that voice coming back and is an important experience to release. What is certain is when you keep on this track, things will unfold in ways you and I are not equipped to imagine. Remember, the same field of potential that created black holes and the human body is your partner in this adventure. And progressing on this journey will inevitably bring you closer to your true self.

Living in Your True Self

As you now know, your true self is an integral part of the universe. Since the universe encompasses everything, a major indication that you are moving in the right direction is an increase in the compassion and empathy you begin to feel for others. I remember when I first started to sense this. It came up very naturally but occasionally caught me by surprise. It has changed how I react to situations close to and far from me. More empathy may sound very positive, and from an ethical perspective, it certainly is, but from personal experience, it can be a double-edged sword. Let me explain.

A couple of years ago, a friend had a colleague who had decided to end their own life. I had met this person briefly before but didn't know them personally. They were young, with a wife and two young kids. Obviously, most reasonable people would feel compassion and empathy for this man and his close ones. My reaction, however, was surprisingly potent. Hearing the news, I felt extremely emotional, almost to tears. I felt physically sick for a couple of days afterward, and I just couldn't stop feeling sadness and loss for this man. I kept replaying what he must have gone through in the days leading up to his decision and was constantly thinking about how I could have intervened to prevent this (even though he probably didn't even know who I was).

This reaction was significantly more emotionally charged than I would have predicted. I now feel more extreme emotional and physical responses when I see an ambulance pass by with sirens on or when I walk past a homeless person in the street. I am at once grateful for these feelings and challenged in dealing with them, but in the final analysis, the fact I have them is a sure sign I'm on the right track.

Being more empathetic in dealing with people has been a gift I didn't expect. I feel I can "put myself in other's shoes" much more easily now, especially dealing with challenging people. Since I know deep down that we're the same being and have the same challenges with the same illusory self often leading the way, I can manage confrontation from a different place than I used to. Ironically when I manage to do this, the relationship with the challenging person has not only improved but, on several occasions, has flipped over to a much closer relationship than before.

One final observation I found in my journey is that *fear* played a starring role for me in the early stages, as it may do for you. Fear is a strong emotion and a necessary one. Fear drives you to react to situations where your physical body is at risk. Hence it keeps the human body safe and is vital to the evolution of all living things.

Irrational, psychological fear, however, is the main source of sustenance for the Imaginary Me. Created by regrets of the past and unrealistic projections for the future, fear can prevent us from moving forward, even in our journey to wake up to reality and our purpose. Fear of the unknown, fear of change, and fear of failure are strong emotions used frequently by the illusory self. They just so happen to also be the main fear-based emotions that surfaced for me as I progressed through this journey.

Dealing with Fear

Given how potent fear is and the irony that it will probably appear strongest as you start to uncover your true self (I see it as the last throes of the illusory self as it sees its inevitable demise!), I'd like to offer some advice for dealing with it.

By far, most of the time that humans have been on this planet, we have been like most animals today. Driven by the need to survive to reproduce, we have a basic and reactive way to keep our bodies safe. When we, as Neanderthals hundreds of thousands of years ago, heard a sound in the forest at night, there would be a good chance that that noise represented an animal coming to eat us. Hence, we evolved an internal emotion to push us to respond appropriately to keep us from harm. This primordial fear was essential in enabling humans to continue to exist and evolve.

Fast forward to only a few thousand years ago, and those rustlings in the bushes no longer represent a clear and present physical danger to us. We hear the noise in scenarios such as the possibility of losing a job or a relationship. We even hear the noise as things we desire, such as a new car, but fear not having. This is psychological fear and is based on numerous "what if" scenarios that are most often not rooted in the real world. However, our emotional response operates very similarly to the pending pouncing of a tiger a hundred thousand years ago. It kicks in to protect us from harm. The harm might be imaginary in nature but feels very real at the time.

In truth, fear, regardless of what caused it to appear, is a safety mechanism. It is trying to protect us. It is just as much a natural part of us as our arms, legs, and mind. As such, we shouldn't try to suppress or criticize any feelings of fear. Rather seek to understand the source of the emotion and decide whether to buy into it or not. Most often than not, our psychological fears are truly imaginary.

Remember the Cornell University study from Chapter 2? Researchers there asked participants to write down their worries over an extended period. They found that 85 percent of what the group worried about never happened, and in the 15 percent that did happen, 79 percent discovered they could handle the situation much better than anticipated. *This means that 97 percent of what we worry about is fiction or exaggeration.*

As in the Stone Age, physical fear today still represents pending danger and usually solicits an autonomous physical response that is the same for all of us. You will fear a car hurtling toward you, and your body instinctively gets out of the way; you don't even think about it. I'd react the same, as would every member of my family and friends.

However, psychological fear is very personal. I may fear losing my job. Someone else may be fine with that but deeply fears losing a relationship. Why does each of us have different triggers for irrational fear? It is because our fears are based on the unique combination of experiences that have happened to us on our journey through life.

As we've discussed, whenever we experience things we don't like, we tend to suppress them, keeping them hidden away in the dark so we don't have to experience them again. As we accumulate more and more of these shadows, they trigger our fear responses. I say accumulation because often, we can't tie our psychological fear of something to one episode in our lives. Hence, we might often hear ourselves and others referring to a traumatic event in the past still impacting us. For example, "I argued with my mother when I was twelve, and she threatened to leave me. Now I fear that everyone in my life will eventually leave me all alone in the world." Of course, that can happen, but we more often fear something and have no idea why. It's a complex combination of these rustling bushes that form a subconscious fear of something particular to you.

For example, for as long as I can remember, I've had irrational fears of losing all my possessions and being homeless. I often see homeless people on the street and think, *"That will be me one day."* But I have been lucky enough to always be able to get by, sometimes very comfortably, as have my family. So I have no rational source for that fear. However, the fear *is there*, and it is powerful. It often feels like a physical thing in my body and sometimes emerges even without an external trigger. I know it has influenced the direction of my life many times. I have taken jobs that I didn't really want just so that I can feel financially safe. I know I am not alone in this. In fact, I'd argue that everyone has some irrational fear they can't really explain.

These feelings of fear are real emotions that are here for a reason. Rather than looking at fear as something that you must tolerate, perhaps become a little more inquisitive. Since the reason why any type of fear exists in the first place is as a protection mechanism, then even irrational, psychological fear must have some positive end. Maybe think about fear as a guidepost to understanding a deeper part of yourself. Psychological fear could be compared to a light shining on the trapped experience, to expose it, to really see it so that you can let it go. Remember, these fears have been formed by suppressed experiences throughout our lives. What if the fear response is a signal to look at these trapped experiences, acknowledge their existence, then release them from their suppression?

I'm not saying that doing this will immediately bring relief from any or all of your fears, but perhaps having a different perspective might change the emotional response it creates. Finding these shadows and shining this light of awareness on them is one of the reasons why we're here. To learn from our experiences, to take on the challenge of understanding them, and to let them go. In doing this, we learn about ourselves and grow into the person we were always meant to be.

In summary, fear is our friend! Its purpose is to help protect us, and therefore it is necessary. It's an intimate part of who we are,

We ARE Awareness

and although the feeling itself can be uncomfortable, know that it's here for a reason, and that reason is always positive.

So what can you do to understand your fearful friend? The first step is to acknowledge that fear is real, it's here, and it's not out to get us. When you understand that to be your truth, you can begin feeling into the emotion. Inquiring into these feelings cannot be read on a page. It's something that must be experienced. But the bottom-line is don't suppress fear. Welcome it and try to understand why it's rustling in the bushes. Let's spend a couple minutes doing that right now.

Don't suppress fear. Welcome it and try to understand why it's rustling in the bushes.

Take a few moments to relax and become still. Think of a scenario that triggers a fearful emotion you want to understand more. It's probably a good idea to work with a low-energy emotion first; let's not try to boil the ocean on the first try! When you feel fear, sense it as a physical sensation in your body. Where is it? It could be in your chest, stomach, neck, or face—this varies from person to person. When you can feel the physical sensation associated with the fear, sink into that physical feeling. Don't think about it, don't judge it, just feel it deeply. Go as deep as you can into it. Perhaps breathe into it.

Eventually, you may learn to recognize fear as just a fluctuation of energy inside you. It's nothing to be afraid of, nothing to try to get rid of. It's just energy in the same way that feeling excited is energetic. Now try to release that energy. Just let the energy associated with the feeling drop or float away. You may feel physically lighter as a result. If you can, try to sense what's left when this energy has been released. What or who was the entity that was experiencing that feeling of fear? No need to be able to answer that question. Most of us can't. Just considering it is enough for now. Spend more time if you like on this excursion, then come back!

And that's it. Right there, you've shone a light on an experience trapped in the shadows. Don't expect any answers or insights, and don't expect the feeling of fear to be eliminated immediately. In fact, we never seek to eliminate fear, just to understand it. To sense the one experiencing it, rather than feeling we are the fear itself. That alone reduces its emotional energy, and the corresponding level of discomfort will show you there is still more work to be done. But by doing this exercise frequently, you'll soon understand why you have that fear. These insights will come quite unexpectedly and may be surprising. You're peeling back layers of experience, and as that happens, you'll gradually see the genesis of the fear. That's a nice feeling, trust me!

Finally, regarding fear, know that these internal fearful energies are transmuted into the higher energies of peace and happiness simply by letting them go. I now look at these resistant emotions firstly with respect and secondly as sustenance. They are there to help us convert those unwanted and unneeded emotions into more potent energies that are aligned with our purpose. Believe me, you will (and should) experience fear during waking up. Welcome it, respect it, and convert it!

Recognizing the Moment

The techniques discussed in this chapter have been used in spiritual practices in one form or another for many years. This should give you some degree of confidence that they are effective. Again, I ask that you embark on these practices and see how they work for you. Keep an open mind and heart and be diligent in your efforts. Maybe make a pact with yourself that you will stick to recognizing "in the moment" growth opportunities, and perhaps practice letting go of past trapped emotions once a day for a month and see how it affects you.

If you ever have the desire to explore spiritual practices in more depth, you will come to realize, as I did, that what we've shared together in this chapter is the essence of all spiritual teachings. Being spiritual is not about trying to attain nirvana or enlightenment. It is simply about living with the illusory self while living your true purpose.

This is your life. Nothing is more important. This is *the reason* why you've been put on this planet at this time. You were meant to experience life fully rather than "get through it," as most people do.

The next chapter continues exploring techniques you can use to help dissolve the illusory self, see your true self more clearly, and grow your sense of purpose.

Chapter 8

More Cloud-Clearing Practices

How Do We Reset Reality?

Before we look at some of the more popular and effective meditation techniques and other cloud-clearing practices to help close the disillusionment gap, let's reset the context of our underlying goals.

Reality Recap

Early in this book, we saw through direct experience how we can't possibly be the things we are aware of in our lives, namely our physical bodies, objects we see, our thoughts, or our emotions. All these things change constantly throughout our lives, yet we have a sense of a continuous "me" throughout. How do we know they change? We know because there is an observer present that is always aware of what's happening. Beneath the busyness of thinking and feeling, we *are* this awareness. It's all we've ever been. It never changes, and it's the same for every human being that has ever lived. This awareness is not just personal; it's universal. The same observer aware of your pain is also aware of the supermassive black hole at the center of our galaxy.

Cloudless Reality

The nature of this awareness is happiness and wholeness. If we could live with this awareness completely, there would be no suffering, discontent, unease, or sense of separation. Most of us, however, don't experience our lives this way. Rather we experience an almost constant feeling of unease with occasional spikes of intense happiness and joy and crushing sadness and suffering. The only reason we don't experience happiness every moment is that we have forgotten our real selves and become so invested in objects, thoughts, and feelings, that we believe ourselves to be those things. The more we can see these experiences for what they are and live as the *awareness* of them, the more we will cease to feel these negative emotions.

Just as with the letting go practices we explored in the previous chapter, some simple practices can increase your awareness of the present moment and allow you to get in touch with your true self again. So, if you're ready, let's start.

Developing Awareness

Meditation and several other techniques we'll discuss in this chapter focus on reversing the process that got us here. If the cause of our suffering focuses on what we experience rather than the real me who is aware of it, let's instead focus on the awareness itself. For example, when we say, "I am tired," we literally mean it. We ARE tired. What does that mean? You can't possibly BE a thing called tired or any other feeling. If your mood changed from tired to sad, would you then claim that you are no longer a thing called tired but now something entirely different called sad? You, *yourself*, have now changed. This doesn't seem intuitive. Let's look

More Cloud-Clearing Practices

at these "I am" statements in a different way.

When we say, "I am tired," let's focus on the "I am" rather than the "tired." If we separate the two parts of the statement, it becomes apparent that there is an "I" that is experiencing the emotion of being tired. Built into our very language is the clear delineation between the act of observation and the experience being observed. "I see the moon," "I hear the birds," "I think I'm going home now," and "I feel confident." The essence of meditation is to spend time reflecting on the awareness that is doing the experiencing. As we've said, this awareness is who you really are. It's the same "I" that is aware of everything in the universe, since you and the universe are the same thing. Getting closer to sensing this awareness then is literally getting closer to yourself. This isn't about working to *find* the "I". It's more a case of carving out time to remember that we

> *We return to our true state when we remember we are the observer, even for a few minutes. This is meditation.*

are the awareness and not the things we are aware of. Most of the time we forget this, as the mind dominates our days and distracts us. We return to our true state when we remember we are the observer, even for a few minutes. This is meditation.

We start by quieting that voice inside that constantly presents stories, objects, thoughts, and emotions. By giving yourself some time to quieten this voice, you'll naturally feel more relaxed and focused. It's not always easy to do. The mind, driven by the illusory self, was created to do the opposite of what you're trying to do. Its very nature is distraction, so attempting to quieten it down

Cloudless Reality

will initially feel like an effort. The good news is there are tried and tested techniques practiced for thousands of years that can be employed to do this. All you need is the *will* to do it.

If you consider the process of "letting go" in the previous chapter, its purpose is to dissolve the clouds that obscure the view of the sky. Meditation practices do the same, but in a pre-planned situation rather than in the moment. As such, these practices are akin to a training session to work out the muscles of cloud-busting for you to use in your day-to-day activities.

Let's look at some methods to achieve this. This is by no means a complete list. Feel free to find a method that works for you. The important point is that being mindful of what's happening inside you is one of the most impactful things you can do to investigate your true nature.

You'll eventually get to a point in meditation that the clouds clear to a point where you can start to investigate the sky.

Think of it as checking on the weather inside. Do you have a relatively blue sky today? Are there a few thunderclouds around? By doing this, you can differentiate the illusory self from your true self, then dissolve those clouds. You'll eventually get to a point in meditation that the clouds clear to a point where you can start to investigate the sky. Then things get interesting.

Silent Meditation

The following excursion requires you to settle, for as little as 5 minutes, either sitting or lying down (sitting is preferable as lying down could bring on sleep!). As you become more accustomed to meditation and perhaps make it a daily practice, extend the time to around 30 minutes. Spending just 5 minutes on this exercise will do, though; try it now.

Find a time and place where you'll be undisturbed. Ideally, sit on a chair with your feet on the floor and your hands resting upward on your lap. Now you're ready:

Close your eyes, take a few deep breaths, and relax your body. You will immediately hear your inner voice resisting. Of course, it's resisting, it knows you're trying to silence it, and it won't like it one bit. Rather than be drawn into its objections, focus on something else called your anchor. Ideally, the anchor is something that you can put your mind to work on that keeps it focused but won't bring up any associated thoughts and feelings. Remain here for your allotted time and enjoy the stillness of the present moment.

Most people choose the breath as their anchor. The breath is always there, is rhythmic, and pervades your entire body. Focus on the breath intensely for several deep breaths and continue to do this for as long as you can. Alternatively, you could choose your heartbeat, a part of your body, or even a sound. Whatever you choose, really try to feel it intensely.

Cloudless Reality

When you first start a meditation practice, I guarantee your mind will try to pull you away from the anchor and will succeed many times. It will talk about what you have planned for dinner, ask are the kids okay, tell you that your legs are hurting, and this meditation is all silly stuff, and many more creative comments, believe me! When you realize that has happened, gradually return to your chosen anchor. Don't be critical, judgmental, or angry at the voice. Remember, it is a part of you. It's trying to protect you, and you created it, so be kind. Be aware that any emotional reaction to the voice will just take you away from your anchor and will strengthen the distraction.

This isn't a battle, just a gentle acknowledgment and a return to the anchor. The practice is to keep doing this for the time you've given yourself. Just watching what's happening within and focusing on the anchor. This will be difficult at first, but trust me, this gets easier each time you try. Please don't aim for an enlightened feeling or flashing lights and angels. That typically will not happen. Meditation is a very practical (hence "practice') way to get to know the real you.

Simple meditation doesn't require that you go looking for the "I" (although there are more advanced techniques that do). If you're new to meditation, simply watching what's going on inside as you move back and forth between the mind's distractions and your anchor is an extremely effective practice. Know that there is no such thing as a "bad" meditation. The mere fact that you have been able to sit and attempt to look inwards is something that most people never do in their entire lives. If you come out

More Cloud-Clearing Practices

of meditation and think, "That was a waste of time. My mind was just racing the whole time." Congratulations! How did you know that your mind was racing?

As you practice this, you'll notice periods, maybe very short initially, where the voice completely subsides, and there are no thoughts or feelings. It's difficult to describe this experience since it will be unique to everyone but suffice it to say once you do experience no-mind, you'll want to experience it again! When there are no thoughts, there are no words you can use to describe the experience. Words like stillness, silence, peace, happiness, contentment, void, and infinite are perhaps pointers to it, but whatever it is for you, it will be positive. Why positive? Because when the mind is still, the clouds move away, and you start to see glimpses of your sky, and we all know that that default state is happiness. Although you may not experience happiness initially, you should start to at least feel a reduction or cessation in the underlying unease. For me, it feels like a weight is being lifted from me. All those stories that become the dial tone of our days just leave you, and what you're left with is a feeling of lightness.

Each time you do this practice, your mind will understand what's going on and, although never immediately obedient, will tend to quieten down more quickly and for longer periods. As more of the raw awareness is revealed, the more you start to understand who you are, why you're here, and what your purpose in life is. Don't go looking for those things. This is much more a revealing of what's always been there rather than a search. Anxiously seeking it has the reverse effect. You're indicating to yourself that you don't have something when you seek to find it. Your role is to sit back and clear those clouds. Nature will take care of the rest.

Meditation is one of the most reverential acts you can perform as a self-conscious being. Many religions and spiritual teachings consider meditation a sacred practice and perform rituals before and afterward as an act of deference (although this is not needed in your practice). Even prayer could be considered a form of meditation, the similarities being quite evident. If we think about what's happening in meditation, we are experiencing ourselves. It's as close as possible to the "I" we've discussed. Since we now understand this "I" is the universe, the act of meditation is the act of the universe experiencing itself. As such, it is the most spiritual and the most natural practice to engage in as a self-aware part of the universe. Even if you're not spiritually driven, meditation is now prescribed for many mental health ailments, including depression and addiction.

The following alternatives to meditation are all based on the same technique presented above, with some slight differences.

Guided Meditation

As the title suggests, guided meditation includes another person (live or a recording) providing vocalization throughout the meditation, typically based on a certain subject. Such subjects could be conquering fear, overcoming anxieties, finding your purpose, and how to relax. In fact, no topic is off-limits in guided meditation. The meditator focuses on the voice and any mental images that come up from the vocalization of the guide rather than the breath. The outcome is very similar to silent meditation but

More Cloud-Clearing Practices

is typically rooted in the topic of the meditation session. The aim of guided meditation is to use the quietening of the illusory voice as an opportunity to speak directly to your true self on a certain topic. When the mind is quiet, and the awareness is clear, you have a direct line to yourself.

If you go to YouTube or use Spotify, you'll find a range of guided visualizations. Pick one that appeals, pop your buds, and tune in to experience no-mind. You'll probably feel more relaxed and at peace, so this is a great way to start or end the day.

Visual and Auditory Meditation

This is like silent meditation, but rather than focusing on an anchor, the focus is on either an image held in the mind or a word or statement repeated silently or aloud (sometimes referred to as a mantra). The image could be connected to a particular intention for the meditation, perhaps the face of a loved one for a meditation on love or a positive reinforcement statement such as "I am courageous." The outcome is very similar to guided meditation, being rooted in the topic of the meditation session. Again, the aim of visual and mantra meditation is to use the quietening of the illusory voice to speak directly to your true self.

Mindfulness

Mindfulness is an important method to bring the same attention in meditation to your everyday life. If meditation is the training session, mindfulness is the game. Rather than selecting a time and place to practice meditation, mindfulness helps integrate the inner

Cloudless Reality

focus we have in meditation with our everyday tasks. Otherwise, mundane activities, such as making a coffee or brushing our teeth, are done with an intense focus on the act itself. No attention is paid to thoughts and feelings that typically come and go during these repetitive tasks, just the task itself.

I tend to seek out activities where my mind would typically wander. For me, the shower is fertile ground for my mind to conjure up some quite creative stories. In the few minutes it takes to shower, I can find a cure for cancer, imagine myself on the moon, craft an email, watch a conversation between two voices about what shirt I should wear today, and finish it off with a criticism of how I haven't cleaned this shower for a while.

Next time you have a shower, listen to yourself. After a while of practicing mindfulness meditation, it becomes a fun game to just listen in non-judgmentally to what's going on inside. I often find myself laughing in the shower nowadays! Alternatively, I often just focus on the feel of the water on my skin. The solid foundation of the shower floor on my feet and how that makes the soles of my feet feel. Or sometimes, just focus on the breath as a reliable anchor. It is surprising how much more enjoyable everyday activities can be when immersed in them.

Mindfulness can be done anywhere and at any time and will be effective for any task where your mind typically wanders.

Mindfulness can be done anywhere and at any time and will be effective for any task where your mind typically wanders. If you're trying to figure out a balance sheet for your company, that task

More Cloud-Clearing Practices

won't be as effective for mindfulness practice! The aim is to use the time when your mind would usually wander to train yourself to bring attention back to something real, to the present moment activity you're engaged in.

> Look for opportunities to get into a mindful state. Especially any time you feel "bored'. Waiting in line at the checkout. Sitting in the doctor's office for an appointment. All great opportunities to go inwards and spend time there. You'll find, not surprisingly, that time will move faster when you pull yourself out of the time-bound illusory mind. By doing this as often as possible, you're training yourself to pull back when a situation arises that could generate an emotional response (the doctor says it'll be another 30 minutes, sorry!).

By taking your attention off the illusory commentary as often as you can, not only are you helping to clear your sky, but you are also spending more time in the present moment. Both actions bring you closer to yourself and, over time, will rebalance your inner state to be less illusion and more real. With that comes a more rational, peaceful, and, yes, happy you.

There is now overwhelming evidence that mindfulness can be a key contributor to stress and anxiety reduction, and as such, many institutions are now offering mindfulness courses. I find the combination of mindfulness over the day, with a fixed time for a meditation session, is most effective. Again, I urge you to try both and see what works for you.

Staying the Moment

Coming back to our discussion on the nature of time from Chapter 5. Your true nature is awareness, as is the true nature of the universe. Since awareness is void of any experience, is it also void of time. We also concluded logically and experientially that the present moment can only exist in zero time. So logically, the closer you get to the present moment, the closer you are to universal awareness. The closer you are to the real you.

Similar to mindfulness, "being in the moment" is just that. Whatever the present moment is, embrace it completely, "as if you had chosen it," as Eckhart Tolle[21] would say.

> Waiting for a bus, sitting at a red light, walking in the woods. Whenever you can, just take a step back and be there with no judgment, no thoughts, and no emotions. Just be there. Watch the people waiting with you at the bus stop, look at the brightness of the red traffic light, and examine intently the leaves on a tree in the woods. The aim is to remove time from your experience. Just be in this very moment. Perhaps try to drill down into the moment, reducing it as we did in Chapter 5. It is

More Cloud-Clearing Practices

one second, half a second, the blink of an eye? See how far you can drill into the moment. The present moment isn't in time, so taking this journey down the rabbit hole can be quite interesting!

You could also just watch thoughts and emotions as they come up in the present moment. It's important here, however, not to get caught up in them. It's much easier to look at a leaf non-judgmentally than your feelings about it. Thoughts and feelings tend to be much stickier. However, if you have been practicing meditation for a while, it is possible to include your thoughts and feelings in the moment as just other objects to observe with no attachment. If a feeling of regret surfaces, for example, it must be observed, as would the leaf. If not, you will be pulled into mind.

With present-moment awareness, you are interrupting the temporal flow of charged thoughts and feelings and stepping outside to experience things as they are now. You are momentarily looking through the eyes of that four-year-old again through the eyes of the real you.

As you do this more often, you'll feel your thoughts starting to quieten immediately. You can't be fully in the moment and attached to thinking or feeling at the same time. Try it; it's impossible. Your body will start to naturally relax. Because the illusory self only exists in time, the closer you get to the present moment (no time), the more the illusory self evaporates, revealing the real you.

Staying in the moment is especially useful in releasing stored emotions and experiences, as discussed in Chapter 7. If you can recognize a situation in the moment where there could be a potential trigger of an unwanted experience, using this practice helps interrupt the temporal flow and buys you precious time to relax and release (see below).

Body Awareness

The two things most intimate to us are the body and the mind. During meditation, we aim to subdue the busy mind to get closer to stillness. The body itself can therefore be used as a focus in meditation. We've already talked about the breath and the heartbeat as powerful anchors, but we can use the body more broadly in this respect too. Contemplation of the innate intelligence of the body, from the breath to the heartbeat, to every one of the hundred trillion cells doing its thing, is an effective way to keep the mind focused. I also find it a means to "check in" on the body. Identifying areas that need attention and being grateful for this amazing machine we get to use.

A powerful technique, and one used frequently in mindfulness exercises, is the body scan. Try it now.

> Take your time doing this. Some scan sessions can take 30–45 minutes to complete but go at a pace that you feel comfortable with.
>
> Relax into a silent meditation, perhaps using your breath as an anchor before moving your focus to either

More Cloud-Clearing Practices

the top or the bottom of your body. Using the breath to guide you, put all your attention on each body part as you move up or down the entire body. Start from the tips of your toes and focus on each part of your body until you reach the crown of your head. All the while, try to remain intensely focused on each body part. And it may help to visualize the muscles, tendons, blood vessels, and skin that compose the area in focus.

What I've found in doing body scans for several years is threefold. First, by intently focusing on the body, you give the mind something to do other than argue and fight about the situation. Although the mind isn't totally quiet, it is singularly focused, which is a huge benefit. Second, in my journey through the body, I often feel a sense of the intelligence there. I can see how little I control what's happening, so I step back and watch the show. It feels liberating but with a heavy dose of humility and awe. Finally, having completed the scan, I occasionally feel a residual sense of wholeness inside, like I've just witnessed a very complex orchestra playing the best composition I've ever heard.

Body focus can also be used in the management of physical pain. Various guided meditations can help focus on a particular area of the body that needs attention. Often, acknowledging the pain, being "okay" with it, and feeling compassion for the affected area can help speed up the recovery process. I'm not advocating using meditation instead of traditional medical treatment, but from my experience, it certainly helps, both physically and psychologically.

Cloudless Reality

Self-Inquiry

Self-inquiry is a more advanced meditation technique that proceeds from a state where the mind is already quiet (perhaps through a silent meditation). When you have a sense of the awareness inside, you begin to investigate precisely what this awareness is by asking yourself, "Who Am I?" This is more an act of gentle curiosity than a demand for an answer. Approaching this like a curious toddler might look at their reflection for the first time.

Self-inquiry was popularized by Ramana Maharshi in the early 1940s and is considered one of the most effective methods to experience our inner reality. Let's try it now.

It is best to progress through a few meditation practices before taking this on since self-inquiry can only begin from a place of inner stillness.

1. Move into a relaxed meditation state. Focus on your anchor and gradually quieten the mind.
2. Now turn your attention to the one who is observing anything that is there. What is present could be more mind chatter; it could be a physical feeling in the body due to an emotion. Whatever it is, don't focus on the object of observation itself. Just focus

More Cloud-Clearing Practices

on being aware of whoever is watching.
3. Then ask, "Who am I?"
4. Try to look for a source of your awareness. Can you find an entity somewhere in there that is watching? Perhaps it has a location in or outside the body? Maybe it has a shape, a size, a boundary, a weight, and a personality to it. Give yourself some time to really contemplate this. It may be a little difficult initially, but it gets easier each time. I tend to imagine traversing up a chain, trying to get to the topmost point where I assume the source exists.
5. Now pull back your focus and return to your anchor to ground yourself again in the present moment.
6. When you're ready, do the same exercise, but now focus on the thoughts and emotions that come up, not on the awareness that observes them. Don't get attached to them. Just observe them. Then ask, "Where are these experiences coming from?' Try to look for a source of the thought or feeling. Again, perhaps these have a location in or outside the body? Maybe they have a shape, a size, a boundary, a weight, a personality.

Spend as much time as you feel comfortable doing this exercise. Perhaps alternate between finding the source of the observer and the source of the thoughts and emotions.

Everyone's experience is different, but my insights from performing self-inquiry several times were surprising, but I sensed the same things each time.

- Whatever it is that is aware of my thoughts and feelings seems to have no location, no size or shape, no mass, and no place in time. It's more a sense than a thing.
- Whatever the source of my thoughts and feelings seems to have no location either. No size or shape, no mass, no place in time. Thoughts and feelings seem to come from nowhere, then sink back to nowhere. It's more a sense than a thing.
- Although I couldn't identify a place or object for either, I am always convinced they arise from the same place.

Tracing back the source of awareness as far as I could and then tracing the source of the objects of awareness leads me to the same place. What that place is, I can't say. Maybe we simply cannot know that. Through self-inquiry, I know that awareness and the objects in awareness are the same. It's all one. Try it if you feel ready. I can't say you'll experience the same things I did, and I hope not to have influenced you in that regard, but if you're practicing correct meditation, your truth will come to you too.

Relaxing and Releasing

As discussed at length in Chapter 7, this is perhaps one of the most effective ways to clear away the emotional blockages within and reduce the resistance we feel. Whether this is applied "in the moment" to situations that cause negative emotions to arise unexpectedly, or if they surface naturally on their own, or perhaps you consciously try to find them, the relaxing and releasing process is the same; here it is.

I've included the checklist and explanation of the technique from Chapter 7 as a reminder of how to look at any of the three scenarios above that create an emotional response.

1. This is the universe unfolding as it should; nothing to do with you.
2. We are all interconnected, so you are a part of this experience. It's not happening "to you'. Your response to this right now will have an impact far beyond anything you can imagine.
3. If the reaction involves another person, you know you are part of the same "I." In the truest sense, you are engaging with yourself.
4. The present moment is the most precious thing that exists in the universe. Actually, it's the only thing! Do you want to waste it on this experience?
5. There are an infinite number of things going on in the universe right now; why are you so concerned about this one?
6. Now you know that you may store this inside of you, do you really want that?

Since the reason why stored experiences are trapped in there is that you decided to suppress them, then the way to release them is to do the opposite. Regardless of how emotionally charged the experience is, the first thing to do after identifying them is to welcome them. This sounds counterintuitive, but trust me, this is a powerful way to let them go. Allow yourself to feel the emotion. Don't think about the thoughts that may come up in reaction to the emotion or memory; focus on the feeling.

If you physically react to the emotion (tightness in the chest, butterflies in the stomach), feel those too. Try to see them as they are, an intimate part of you that is desperate for release. Maybe imagine them holding a hand for you to grab and pull up and out of their prison. As they come up, welcome them. I sometimes smile during this process, occasionally even holding out my arms to physically welcome them up. It can also be helpful to imagine a physical space around the feelings. They've been suppressed for so long it can be liberating to feel that space. When you feel that you're sitting with them, not thinking, not judging, just with them, then physically relax your entire body and,

Let them go.

Imagine them floating out of your body or breathing them out. It doesn't matter how you do this; just know that letting them go is imbued with positivity, respect, and lightness. Certainly not pushing or forcing anything. Remember, they want to go; you're just letting them do their natural thing.

Try to do this with an open heart, letting whatever happens just happen, and I guarantee you will start to feel physically lighter. You can do this as often as you wish, with as many trapped experiences and emotions as you want to; just be genuine each time. Some more powerful trapped feelings may take many "releases" before they leave, but trust me, be patient, and they will leave.

As with any of the techniques above, the more you practice relaxing and releasing, the more you will cleanse yourself of past stored emotions. As the trapped emotions are removed, the only thing left is what's always been there, your true self. That is when the real spiritual journey can begin. When the miracles start to happen.

As Nature Intended

I hope you have found this summary of some of the most effective techniques helpful. By integrating some of these practices into your life and understanding them in the context of our alternative way of looking at the world, you will feel the benefit. You are doing what nature intended you to do.

If you recall our discussion on interconnectedness in Chapter 5, since everything is connected, then as you work with these practices, you are creating an impact somewhere else in the universal plane. As Buddha said:

> "The happiness of one depends upon the happiness of all, and the happiness of all depends upon the happiness of one."

In that vein, then, let's now examine some of the broader implications of this way of living. What would our world be like if many of us could experience more of that river flowing, and how can we make moves to get ourselves there? Let's look at some of these broader implications in the next chapter.

Chapter 9

Reality Redesigned

What Is the Broader Impact of this Worldview?

In the preceding chapters, we examined the human condition of incompleteness, unease, and suffering, occasionally interspersed with moments of peace, joy, and happiness. We looked at that voice inside our heads and its reason for existing. We saw that our real life is akin to the sky obscured by clouds, and the way through this is to let the clouds pass by without regard, seeing more and more sky. We looked at techniques to clear away those clouds, providing a clearer picture of our true selves and place in the world. We then concluded our journey by examining our individual purpose in life and how that is part of an incomprehensibly greater universal unfolding. Everything discussed thus far has purposefully focused on the personal. Having established the impact of this view from an individual perspective, let's now look at some of the broader impacts this way of looking at and living life could have across societal, ecological, health, education, and scientific standpoints.

Cloudless Reality

Societal Norms

We've talked at length in the book of the Imaginary Me. That voice within that is driven only to seek and resist and live only in the remembered past or the imagined future. We also saw, through personal experience, that this is truly an illusion. It doesn't exist in and of itself. As well as an illusory personal self, there are illusory personas across societies. These are powerful phantoms, able to wreak havoc on their close collective, such as families and friends, as well as broader societal groups. This is the very source of nationwide conflict. Indeed, any societal act that results in negative outcomes for any is ultimately rooted in the illusory mind. Whether due to geographic, religious, or any other reason, the collective psyche of the illusory persona will defend its position, even if it means the end of the persona itself.

There is little difference between the nature of the personal and the collective illusory selves. They emerge from the same process of suppressing emotions based on the outside world, failing to match our illusory internal desires. The impact of a society-wide illusion, however, is on a much greater scale since the emotional charge required to fuel this persona must be potent enough to influence behavior across personal boundaries. Often the broader illusion is born from one personal illusion, where, given the correct external environment, it can rapidly spread like a virus. From some of the darkest moments in human history to our daily lives, if we look, we can see the similarities clearly.

It's well understood that Hitler's desire to stamp German authority on the world in World War II was fueled by the collective feelings of German frustration at the close of World War I. Although we can speculate that WW2 may not have taken place without the drive of one man, the collective German sentiment at the time contributed to what happened next. Suppressed feelings of defeat and frustration planted seeds within the population, who were receptive when one personal mind started influencing many. Hence was born a collective illusion, feeling separate from every other group, needing to reinforce its authority, and feeling restricted by time. Something had to happen soon to protect this ghost and at any cost. The rest, as we all know, is history.

School bullying is another example where one personal illusion can influence others to create a collective and damaging Imaginary Me. We probably either know of or have directly experienced being bullied.

I was a studious kid at school and was bullied for a time by a group of kids for being a "nerd" (a title I'm more than proud of, by the way!). There were four of these bullies who would target a group of us bookworms. Although the bullying was never violent, it always focused on one point of aggression. These guys hated that we tended to get higher marks in class, whereas their group was usually at the bottom. At the time, I just thought that they hated kids that were different from themselves, but I now see that differently. A collective illusory self had developed within that group of four from a similar frustration of not being "good enough" compared to the rest of the class. To protect itself from harm, that collective persona lashed out at those most diametrically opposite and separate from itself. Taking down the most potent enemy served to reinforce the reason for this collective self to exist, so the bullying emerged and was positively reinforced by the illusion each time.

How about corporate greed? Or even gossiping? These are other instances where it's clear there is a group of people hearing the same false voice and being directed to act in a harmful manner. It's easy to see that these events—and any social event that harms another—are rooted in wanting or not wanting something. The very definition of the illusory self. It is also immersed in a worldly echo chamber of individuality and separateness, where time and resources are limited. In some way, this provides a false justification for the behavior, and so it goes on and on.

Take a moment to recall a situation where there was a difference of opinion between different groups. It could have been your voice against a crowd or a group having a disagreement with another. The disagreement could be about politics, ecology, or anything but religion is always a good one!

As you think through the scenario, maybe take a moment to consider why each side was behaving the way it was. See if you can uncover a deeper sense of a holistic personality within that crowd that seeks to protect itself.

An obvious example for me would be US politics. Without getting into my political inclinations, I can see a collective persona in one major party versus another. I can also cite examples where one side would have to seriously consider whether the other was sane, so far beyond rational thought have the arguments often gotten. Perhaps this is a collective ego just trying to survive rather than a true belief in what's right or wrong for the country. Try to see it for yourself. It is an interesting alternative perspective.

Social media and the advent of the Internet would seem, on the surface, to provide some opportunity for personal and collective illusory selves out there to be more connected. It seems, however, that quite the opposite has transpired. Existing anonymously behind computer and phone screens, our Imaginary Me's can and do wreak havoc on each other, often with little retribution. Rather than increasing our sense of interconnection, technology has made us more separate than ever. We only need to look around a family dinner table or a group of friends in a coffee shop, everyone heads down on their device, to see the sense of individuality is quite possibly at an all-time high in our society.

> *Rather than increasing our sense of interconnection, technology has made us more separate than ever.*

What would the world look like if people really understood their true nature of interconnection and wholeness? Where we understand that anything we do at any point in time can affect others and that the present moment is the most precious thing

Cloudless Reality

we can possess? That every one of us has a purpose, and every purpose is connected to something higher.

If we could collectively "clear the sky of clouds" and experience our true nature, we'd experience a flow of peace, contentment, and creativity. That creativity could lead us to invent and discover things we couldn't even imagine today. Most of the greatest inventions and discoveries, such as Einstein's breakthrough scientific theories, were realized during quiet contemplation, not in bouts of busy thinking. As Einstein himself said, "I never made one of my discoveries through the process of rational thinking." Imagine a world full of Einsteins. All this could be just the tip of the iceberg for humanity if our compassion and creative potential were fully realized.

Realizing this alternative reality seems like a chasm compared to where we are today. Still, if we are to make changes as a society and evolve past this challenging period, we must become curious as to what our other options are. Since the collective Imaginary Me comprises many synchronous personal illusory selves, we must address this challenge from the individual to the collective. Targeting the root will affect the whole tree. We'll talk more about that in the next few sections.

Ecological Drivers

One of the major drives of the illusory mind is the need to accumulate objects to feed a false sense of lack. The same is true of the collective mind. Combine that with a mistaken sense that time is limited, that the world is a mass of separate objects (including ourselves) to be plundered, and right there, we have a lethal combination that results in mass acquisition at all costs.

It seems that we now know exactly what the ultimate cost could be. A planetary-wide illusory self continues to deplete the Earth's resources despite facts being plain to see. We individually acknowledge the inevitability of this but defend our inaction to fix it with a typical illusory statement, "It's beyond my control." This is a supreme example of how powerful the mind can be in the collective. We understand the current situation regarding climate change. Most of us accept the inevitability of its impact if unchecked. Yet we, both individually and collectively, continue to do the very things that will bring about that result.

"The problem will be fixed in the future" is a statement the illusory self makes when there is no answer in the present. As we kick the ecological can down the road, we seek solace in the assumed inevitability of a solution by someone else in the future, but as we know, the future doesn't exist. Remember, the universe is impersonal in nature. Remember, too, that as the Pale Blue Dot photo demonstrates, we are very small in the universal scheme of things. If we are to annihilate ourselves through an ecological catastrophe, the universe will unfold as it always has. That annihilation is just another experience to be had. No one can save us except ourselves.

An understanding not only of our intimate connection to each other but to everything on the planet would simply not allow us to continue along such a perilous path. If we were to "work on ourselves" to minimize the craving and resisting voice to see the true "I" we are, that realm of infinite possibility would open, and our inevitable demise would be reversed.

As more and more of humanity seek to clear their own sky of those clouds and see more clearly their true selves, not only will we not feel the need to plunder as we do today, but the creativity that could be unleashed by the emergence of the true self could deliver a solution to the ecological decline we are in.

Health Matters

At numerous points throughout the book, we conclude that everything is one, from objects, thoughts, emotions, and even time. We investigated the latest scientific findings, where it is now understood that reality is an energy field containing infinite possibilities and requiring a conscious awareness to bring it into reality.

This being the case, our physical bodies are also fields of vibrational energy, albeit with different frequencies to thoughts and emotions. We also know, again from our direct experience, that thoughts and emotions can affect the physical body (tears when sad, butterflies when nervous, etc.) and vice versa (just stub your toe and see).

Given these factors, the impact of this alternative worldview on our personal health, both physical and mental, could be profound. So many experiments have been conducted and books written on the placebo effect[22] that it's now generally accepted that there's a strong mental component to healing. Many drug companies now use the placebo and nocebo effects in their trialing of new drugs to market.

Reality Redesigned

Consider one of the most pervasive physical diseases in the world today. Cancer is a disease where otherwise normal human cells become abnormal and start to reproduce. Cancer isn't the result of some external invader infecting our bodies, such as Covid or influenza. It is literally our own cells attacking our bodies. Cancer cells differ from normal cells[23] in a few key ways:

- They grow without the body's natural signals telling them to grow. Normal cells only grow when they receive such signals.
- They ignore signals that normally tell cells to stop dividing or to die.
- They invade other areas of the body. Normal cells do not move around the body.
- They tell blood vessels to grow toward the tumors they create, keeping them alive.
- They can hide themselves from the immune system (which is designed to fight abnormality).

There seems to be an intelligence driving these cells to attack their own. They do this even though the result could be the ultimate destruction of the body. Does this sound familiar? We know that the intelligence within our bodies is inconceivable to us, yet this intelligence is often used against us. We don't know exactly why this happens, but we do know it can happen to any of us. We also know that the same intelligence that drives our hearts to beat and cancer cells to attack is the same intelligence that drives the universe. There is only one intelligence.

Pure conjecture on my part, but what if we considered the

natural intelligence of the body analogous to our true selves and the abnormal intelligence just another manifestation of the illusory mind, but at a much deeper level? Given our alternative model of reality as all minds, abnormal human cells are just as much mind stuff as our thoughts. I'm not saying we can now claim to understand the mechanics of cancer; far from it. I suggest an alternative way of looking at what is happening at this deeper level of intelligence rather than the mostly physicalist way we look at it today.

From that view, we could contemplate complementary courses of treatment that use the integrated mind and body to reverse the course of some of these dreadful diseases. Even the word disease (dis-ease, not at ease) seems to imply a deeper analogy to our higher-level feelings of unease. Undoubtedly, strides have been made in the introduction of mind-centric practices into the treatment of many physical ailments. However, we are a very short distance along that path. When more mainstream methods of healthcare focus as much on the mental as the purely physical, we can move more quickly to a place where patients can contribute to their own healing. There are too many examples of the role of the mind in the healing process now for it to be ignored. In a report published in 2017 in *The British Medical Journal*, researchers at Stanford University called for more healthcare providers to emphasize the importance of individual mindsets in healing.

> *"The placebo effect isn't some mysterious response to a sugar pill. It is the robust and measurable effect of three components:*

the body's natural ability to heal, the patient mindset, and the social context. When we start to see the placebo effect for what it really is, we can stop discounting it as medically superfluous and can work to deliberately harness its underlying components to improve health care."[24]

Alia Crum, Ph.D., assistant professor
of psychology, Stanford University

Perhaps the most significant impact of the conscious-only worldview on health is that of mental health. The mental health condition of humanity today is in turmoil. From gun violence to substance abuse to suicide and myriad other symptoms, we are about as far from our true selves as we could imagine, and it's not difficult to see why. The individual and societal illusory self has grown in stealth and power, driven by the materialist view of the world, where separateness and lack are the mainstays of life. Where a primarily nihilistic view of the world is dominant, and life feels pointless and without meaning. The illusory part of our mind only seeks survival. It doesn't need meaning to survive, so it's easy for meaning and purpose to be diminished to the point of elimination. This mind has been allowed to run unchecked for so long that it can now affect its host to the point of destruction (of itself and others).

When we consider typical psychological conditions such as depression, addiction, anxiety, eating disorders, and more severe ailments, including schizophrenia and bipolar, the traditional treatment method is usually a combination of drugs and therapy. Let's use our alternative view of a mind-centric world to see what could be happening here.

We've used various analogies of what it means to be blocked from experiencing your real self. Given your real self is whole, then it cannot have these ailments. It seems logical to claim, then, that these conditions represent a sky almost completely obscured by thunderclouds. We know these clouds are due to past emotional events that have been trapped and stored in the mind, where they are exaggerated and deformed into something more sinister. We also know that these trapped emotions naturally want to be free. All this is analogous to current psychological diagnoses and treatment of mental ailments, where repressed and suppressed memories are exorcised through talk therapy. The patient is often asked to express the past memory in the hope that the associated trapped emotion can be freed. Perhaps augmenting these expressive techniques with a releasing process that doesn't require the direct expression of the memory itself, only letting go of the associated emotion, could prove beneficial.

> *The illusory part of our mind has been allowed to run unchecked for so long that it can now affect its host to the point of destruction (of itself and others).*

Studies have shown that mindfulness techniques could be key in treating depression in adults, both in initial symptoms and in preventing relapse.[25] Combining this treatment with open dialog on the nature of the world as experienced could also affect the condition. Most mental conditions have been created from the patient's prior experience in a primarily material worldview. If they could see an alternative where connection, meaning, and purpose are fundamental, it could go some way to resetting context and assisting in their recovery.

Please know that I'm not suggesting an all-out replacement of traditional treatments for physical and mental ailments but an integration of the old and new that I believe will, over time, become more "new" and less "old."

Education Reform

Changes in collective worldview to the extent covered in this book will take time, but if we are to impact humanity's direction right now, it will have to happen at the root level. Trying to prune branches will not be sufficient to make the necessary societal changes. In Chapter 1, we looked at the changes in early childhood, as the innocence of youth is obscured by society's expectations (when children begin to "eat of the fruit of the tree of knowledge").

It is at this transitional point in our children's education that we can make the most impact. Children must learn early on to work from the inside out rather than the reverse. By helping them understand how our minds work, providing the necessary tools to manage the voice (meditation, mindfulness, etc.), and sharing an alternative view of the world that isn't so nihilistic and mechanistic, we will begin to see change.

Our ability to acquire information almost instantly is starting to show changes in the way recent generations enquire about the world. Young people are more inquisitive and less apt to accept things they are told at face value than previous generations. This is a good thing. Questioning the status quo as it stands now is a necessary part of making the changes needed. However, accessibility to an alternative worldview is sadly lacking in our educational institutions today. Some countries have started building alternative worldviews into their education curriculum and making meditation and mindfulness a natural part of the school day. There are many educators, psychologists, and parents pushing for this to happen sooner rather than later. Let's hope they succeed.

We could then imagine a world where children are taught from an early age a worldview in which they are an integral and interconnected part of nothing less than the universe. That they can impact so many others by even simple actions. That everyone's true nature is rooted in happiness and has a life purpose. They don't have to listen to that illusory voice inside that is beginning to get attention from them. The method of imparting this knowledge must be experiential and not merely academic. As I've tried to do in this book, this knowledge is something that must be experienced if it is to be accepted to the deep level where real change is possible. How can a generation that truly experiences and accepts this worldview then cause harm to another, themselves, or the planet? An idealist view, I admit, but one that we must strive for if our race is to have any hope of longevity.

There is a whole book to be written on the impact of this alternative worldview on education, so we'll leave our surface discussion on this right now. If we can begin to make inroads within our education systems, we will almost certainly experience generational changes in how we treat each other and our homes.

Science vs. Philosophy

With a few notable exceptions, science is rooted in the materialist worldview. That's not surprising, given the prediction power of the material model. It has enabled us to discover and formulate laws of nature that have been vital in the evolution of humanity.

The materialist scientific method, as it has existed for the past few hundred years, is designed to predict the forces of nature, not to know them. For instance, science has become extremely adept at understanding how elementary particles interact using highly complex technology such as the Large Hadron Collider at CERN. Using this sophisticated machine and others, physicists have predicted the behaviors of the very building blocks of matter, applying that knowledge to create ever more sophisticated models of how the universe works. Yet despite some astounding discoveries, we remain in the dark about what constitutes matter itself.

The same could be said of any science-based method today. Earlier in the book, we discussed the challenge of "correlation versus causation" concerning brain activity. Neuroscience has been able to locate, to a high degree of accuracy, areas of the brain associated with body function, such as auditory, visual, and even rational thought. It is not the intention of neuroscience, however, to explain the source of thought or emotion. Hence, we remain with the hard problem of consciousness.

Traditionally, philosophy's domain is understanding the real nature of things, typically through introspection. There was a time when science and philosophy were intertwined ('Natural Philosophy"), with nature's behavior being predicted and introspected. Science and philosophy began to split in the sixteenth century when the scientific method of hypothesis and objective testing against experiments became predominant. Today science is very much in the business of predicting behavior through hypothesis testing, leaving philosophy to the introspection of the world as it really is. Science is predominately objective, and philosophy is subjective.

It is primarily due to this historical split that the materialist model of the universe became entrenched. Rather than just predicting how the world works, science began to assume the predictions were reality. A simple example would be the "discovery" of the atom by John Dalton in 1803. His work was based on meteorology. By studying the behavior of weather patterns, he concluded that rather than a "vast chemical solvent," as was the assumption at the time, gases in the atmosphere act as complex interactions of very small particles. It was later concluded that the entire universe was likewise constructed from individual spheres of matter. Yet to date, no human has ever seen one of these spheres.

I mention this split between science and philosophy to illustrate how the materialist view of the world was able to take hold, despite there being obvious and experiential evidence to the contrary. We have addressed several of those in this book. Since the scientific method required very little introspection, being based solely on what can be proved experimentally, a whole worldview was created that was quite separate from our *experience* of reality.

This is how the material worldview was able to fuel the passions of the illusory self. By validating the world as:

- A place of separate and distinct objects (from atoms to humans).
- We were mere spectators of a mechanistic process with no meaning or telos.
- Where time was a limited resource (since at the end of life, you simply returned to dissipated atoms).

Although hugely successful, this scientific model created quite a sterile and inhuman world. We have been bedazzled by this method's role in our evolution (the internet, the iPhone, Minecraft!), but we also know there's been a price we've paid for this split. Despite all this progress, we've missed something key. Our humanity.

Although we've painted a rather glum picture of the fracturing of natural philosophy, it seems there have been recent, gradual moves in science that open the door to a more introspective approach. There have been many several noted scientists in the recent past beginning to advocate for a consciousness-centric view of reality, which, as we've seen, adequately knits together natural laws with introspection.

Despite all this progress, we've missed something key. Our humanity.

As English astronomer, physicist, and mathematician Sir James Jeans stated in 1940.

> *"The universe begins to look more like a great thought than like a great machine. Mind no longer appears to be an accidental intruder into the realm of matter...*
> *we ought rather hail it as the creator and governor of the realm of matter."*[26]

As more experiments, such as the double slit experiment, present behaviors that cannot be explained without a conscious presence (see Masaru Emoto's experiments on the effect of emotions on water crystals in 2008[27]), we may see a gradual reconvergence of these two methods of investigation into nature.

When that convergence happens, and I very much hope it will, we must retain the objective focus of science but be open to the role of consciousness in both the hypothesis and the results of our theories. When we remove the constraints of a materialist framework, science will become more creative and flexible in its view of reality. This, in turn, would open the door to huge strides in our understanding of the fundamentals of nature. We are intimately combined with nature; hence any understanding we gain about it is always a step towards more understanding of ourselves.

Pros and Cons

Whole books could be written on each topic in this chapter. Still, I hope to have provided a glimpse into the pros and cons of the current and alternative worldviews across societal, ecological, health, education, and scientific standpoints. What is clear in examining these broader impacts is that even just the consideration of a different way of looking at the world could have an impact. If more of us choose to look at the world through experience instead of being taught theories, change can happen. We see small changes emerging from mindfulness in education systems to treatment of physical and mental ailments to scientists looking to conscious agency in their experiments. While such changes may be decades, we must start somewhere.

Chapter 10

Shall We Wrap It Up?

We began our journey by seeking to understand why so many of us feel incomplete and often dissatisfied with our lives, despite having achieved what we believed would bring long-lasting happiness. That sense of disappointment drives many of us to either give up on seeking the meaning of our life, continue to find solace in ultimately unsatisfactory experiences or search for more meaning. Picking up this book puts you in the latter category. Congratulations! This is the most important thing you can do with your time here.

Our Journey

We investigated further why many of us feel this way by experiencing the Imaginary Me, a false persona consisting of thoughts and feelings, typically wrapped in a story and almost always critical. It is this illusory self and its constant storytelling that keeps us from our true selves. The gap between who we are and who this illusion tells us we are is one of the main causes of our disillusionment with life.

Shall We Wrap It Up?

Before examining how we can find more meaning, satisfaction, and connection, we first provided some context by looking at the mainstream view of reality and how it differs from what we experience. A worldview based on individual, material things "out there" creates a sense of separation and lack (of things, of time) and inevitably leads to a desire to pursue experiences we want and to resist any experience we don't want. Not only has this view of reality created personal and social angst in the world, but we also know from our direct experience and recent discoveries in the material-centric sciences that the existing material-only view of the world is incomplete.

Even delving into the experiential nature of time and free will demonstrates that these traditionally de facto assumptions of reality are founded on unstable ground. The present moment is all that exists and all that will ever exist. Paradoxically it also exists in no time. Most of us look to the present moment as something to 'get through', either to get away from an unwanted past or get to an assumed better future. Nothing could be further from the truth! This moment is

> *A worldview based on individual, material things "out there" creates a sense of separation and lack (of things, of time) and inevitably leads to a desire to pursue experiences we want and to resist any experience we don't want.*

all we ever have. There is no past or future except what is remembered or imagined in this moment. Memories and imagination are not real things, yet they dictate our lives.

We looked at the unimaginable complexity of interconnections and how our experiences can impact an infinite number of others, most of which will never be known to us. The universe started from nothing and unfolded from that point. Hence everything that the cosmos is right now was initially interconnected. Remember, we are a part of the universe. We are part of this tapestry of infinite interconnections. What we do, *everything* we do, or don't do, has an impact.

Our alternative view of the world is based on experience since that is the only thing we know for sure exists. The universe, rather than being a complex combination of individuated objects, is more akin to a dream-like experience. The substrate of the universe, which everything is made from, is consciousness. Not that matter *has* consciousness. *Matter is consciousness.* When you see a chair, it is a thought in the mind of nature. Just like a thought, you may have about dinner, just an interpersonal rather than a private thought.

> Our personal consciousness can be likened to a whirlpool in a river of the universal mind. Not separated from the river, but a localized instance of it.

We are here to experience. We were given this amazing body and its five senses to experience the world. We were also given the ability to think and to feel, and the precious gift of introspection, being able to observe ourselves, observing ourselves. All the things that we experience, including objects, thoughts, and feelings, are rendered to us as in a dream where we are the avatar. Our personal consciousness can be likened to a whirlpool in a river of the universal mind. Not separated from the river, but a localized

Shall We Wrap It Up?

instance of it. In this way, the universe can experience itself through us, gaining insights that enable it to unfold. The life of every one of us is thus saturated with purpose and meaning, both our individual meaning and an unfathomable, universal one.

Having established a different way of looking at reality, we ventured to the root of why we feel discontent, separate, and so distant from our purpose in life. The answer can be distilled into two simple reasons.

- We have become so identified with the illusory self within that our true selves have been obscured by this illusion and the stories it tells us. We believe ourselves to be this illusion, considering ourselves victims of our circumstances rather than an integral part of them.
- Since we cannot clearly see our true selves, we cannot get a clear picture of our purpose in life. We may feel it occasionally (as you can occasionally feel the sun behind the clouds), but it is mostly an infrequent spark or a dull yearning in the background of our perception.

You can see from the two points above that if we were to clear away the clouds (illusory experiences) from the sky (our true self), this would address the first point and, consequently, the second. The gap between where we are today and where we should be starts to close, with the natural consequence of "reintegration"— a return to your true self that is complete, interconnected, peaceful, and resting as its default state of happiness.

As the clouds dissipate, you'll feel that dull ache of yearning for

Cloudless Reality

a life filled with meaning and purpose start infiltrating your life. This is your purpose shining through. It never went away but was only ever obscured by the illusory self. By seeing or feeling more clearly what you were always intended to do, you now have an opportunity to use your body, your thoughts, and your feelings as they were intended. To co-create a reality for yourself driven by your purpose. That is how the universe wants to unfold via us. That is the very meaning of life.

Take note that your purpose doesn't have to be lofty. People find purpose in activities that others may think are mundane. It's just as impactful to pursue a purpose in life as a barista as it is to find a cure for cancer. Given the limitless interconnections we've investigated, both scenarios could have a similar impact on the world; we just don't know it.

The gap between where we are today and where we should be starts to close, with the natural consequence of "reintegration"— a return to your true self that is complete, interconnected, peaceful, and resting as its default state of happiness.

So how did we look at addressing the two sources of unease above?

Addressing Unease

Noticing that the voice inside your head is the first and major step to clearing those clouds. The illusory mind only exists because it's hidden. It keeps you busy to avoid being seen! The second step is to nurture the ability to *be* the awareness of objects, thoughts, and

Shall We Wrap It Up?

feelings. Many people who can just do these two things start to see more of the sky and a reduction in their unease. They may even start to feel more strongly about what their purpose in life could be as more of that sky is revealed to them.

Having recognized the voice and felt the self that is the watcher of your experiences, the final step is simply not getting involved with the voice's narrative. When you can recognize the mechanics of that voice, you'll intuitively know what to take seriously and what to ignore. Not suppress. Not push away or cling to. Just pay no attention to it. This keeps your sky clear.

You know you're on the right track by how much unease and discontent you feel. To return to the river analogy, you simply "go with the flow." When you're drifting with the current, you feel at ease, comfortable, and relaxed. When you're against it, life is tough; it's a struggle. Since we know the world is just an experience, if you're experiencing struggle within, it won't be long before it aligns with your external experiences. Then you'll start to recognize situations as ones that create more struggle. As Carl Jung said, "What you resist persists."

> You are the universe, and the universe has your back. Of course, it has; how can it not? It is you!

Don't worry about it. Just let it go. Like falling back into a big fluffy cloud you can't see, we must simply allow ourselves to fall back and trust. You *are* the universe, and the universe has your back. Of course, it has; how can it not? It *is* you!

As you remove those rocks and start to feel the river flow, you will

Cloudless Reality

begin not only to feel a stronger pull to your purpose in life but you'll see indications as to what you should do to get there. Those signposts have always been in your life, but again, you just haven't been able to see them. Now they stare back at you, beckoning you to follow them. That is when the real adventure starts. You may not know where that journey will take you, but rest assured, it is bursting with meaning and purpose.

Thoughts on Passing

When I talk to others about this view of reality, I'm often asked, "What happens at the end of life? What does that mean for us? If we're all part of a universal dream, do we ever wake up? Do our meaning and purpose continue after our physical bodies have gone?"

Let's discuss a little.

I often wonder why the image most often portrayed as death is the Grim Reaper. In his hand, he carries a scythe, an instrument used to harvest crops. Although depicted as the "reaping of the souls of sinners," I'd like to entertain the possibility that at the time of our death, there is a reaping of all our accumulated life experiences. The insights we obtain through introspection throughout our life are "harvested" into the universal consciousness when we die.

To borrow the river and whirlpool metaphor from Chapter 4 once more. When the river's currents dictate, the whirlpool dissipates and merges into the river. When we die, our personal consciousness likewise merges back into the river of universal consciousness.

In Chapter 6, we concluded that the universe is a vibrational field of energy, and we know that energy is conserved in the universe. It cannot be created or destroyed, only changed or merged. Nothing can be wasted. Hence, insights from every second of your life will be re-integrated into the universal mind to contribute to its unfolding, with no waste. Even experiences you do not recall or may not have been aware of will be integrated. In that respect, every second of your life is precious in ways we can't conceive. Much like the character in a dream doesn't really die when you wake up, death is very much like the end of a waking dream. You will not mourn the end of your dream character because you'll realize it was all a dream, and you will awake to your natural self. The universal mind and the personal mind are reunited. You are home.

Since the "essence" of you that we referred to early in the book is core to your personal consciousness, that is conserved and integrated into the broader universal flow upon death. In that regard, the essence of you that the universal "I" has been aware of all your life never really dies.

Rather than a nihilistic view of death as the permanent end of "you," where everything you have experienced is gone when the brain no longer receives oxygen, it seems quite the opposite. This could be a double-edged sword, too, however. Many people, especially if they have had difficult lives, find solace in believing that when they die, that is the end of everything. Materialism has provided relief from believing in heaven and hell, especially hell. The possibility of spending an infinitely long afterlife roasting in fire has been used to control societies for eons. With a purely mechanistic world model, the end of life is *the* end. Period.

In a conscious-only model of the world, we return to the view that the end of life is not the end and that something of "you" remains post-death. What happens to us when we "re-integrate" is forever beyond our ability to know, but we will all experience it eventually. Since we intuit that the natural state of our true self is happiness, I would find it hard personally to imagine the reintegration as being anything other than a positive experience. I guess we shall see!

For most of us, our physical impact on this world will be quickly forgotten. We may find solace in passing our genes on to the next generation, but if we are merely baby-making machines, then it would seem pointless to achieve things in life to have such varied experiences. We are driven to create things, things beyond and not related to the delivery of a giggling bundle of joy. As we now know, these varied experiences are there to be reaped by the universe as it unfolds, contributing to the lives of others in ways we can't imagine.

Not only can this alternative view of death be comforting as you contemplate your own end, but it can make you much more able to deal with loved ones as they approach the end of life too. I've spoken with several nurses at hospice facilities who often report that patients very close to the end of their lives will often enter a period of intense joy and peace before they leave.

In a consciousness-centric world, as we get closer to death in a way that we can contemplate (obviously, this would not apply in a sudden fatal accident, for example), the reintegration to the

Shall We Wrap It Up?

whole has already begun. As the localized consciousness that is the patient begins to merge with the universal mind, the illusory self is shed from the true self, revealing a clear blue sky—the real "I." We know this real "I" has a natural peace and happiness. This is a reversion back to that innocent four-year-old staring at the rose in awe. They are going back home.

Today, and Passing it Forward

What I have found to be the most surprising change in my life as I've started to live it through these new eyes is the impact I see around me. On countless occasions where people have commented that I look healthier, that I'm much happier and more content, and that there is "something different" about me (in a positive way, mostly!). That's not to say I am always in ecstasy, far from it, but I am more at ease with myself and the things around me. I often reflect on my "old" life of constantly needing, judging, fearing, expecting, yearning, and wonder what took me so long to see the truth. Of course, I understand that everything has its time, and it had to happen this way, so I'm grateful.

It is perhaps one of the more impactful signs that in looking at the world this way and working to get a clearer view of my true self, I feel more genuine in my skin. I, like many of us, used to wear many masks, trying to be a different person depending on the situation in front of me. I know now that that was the result of my believing I was an illusionary character, the masks being a desperate reaction from my psyche to find an identity, even if it was a dependent one. That constant changing of one mask to

Cloudless Reality

another was just filling up the sky and obscuring the view, hiding the true face beneath the mask.

Right now, you represent less than 1 percent of the human population that is being true to themselves and seeking answers. I believe that in late, sleepless nights, 100 percent of us acutely feel incomplete to some degree and that each of us, at many times throughout our lives, ponders the answers to life's big questions. This is when most people are immediately overwhelmed by the paranoid illusory self that jumps in, telling a story of how tomorrow's meeting will go and how you need to sleep. Those who can stay with that honesty and those ponderings have created a chink in the doorway to peace they can choose to open.

> *That constant changing of one mask to another was just filling up the sky and obscuring the view, hiding the true face beneath the mask.*

Since our experiences are interconnected, it's my hope that this intuitive way of looking at and living in the world will spread as each of us discovers this truth for ourselves. Many more people are trying to get this message out, but people must be ready and open to accepting a different way of perceiving a well-established world before stepping into it. I believe the most effective way to effect change is to live the new worldview, and it is my hope that if the message in this book resonates with you, you simply live it. People around you will see the difference, which may affect them too. Either way, since every experience we have and every action we take impacts the tapestry of life, just living a life dedicated to clearing the sky and following your purpose will impact the

Shall We Wrap It Up?

world in ways you will never know. Remember, you don't have to renounce anything for this to transform your life. Indeed, living a full life will give you ample opportunity to experience challenges and convert them into happiness. Each time you do this, you're aligning with the real you. You may find that as you see more clearly where you're meant to go, that requires a change in your life. Again, just go with the flow. You will not be presented with anything you can't handle, even if it may seem challenging at the time. When the decision point arrives, you will intuitively know what to do. Remember who you are!

Finally, be patient with yourself as you embark on this adventure. Since you are a part of the unfolding of the universe, the journey you have begun or are continuing along is also part of that unfolding. As such, it has a natural cadence to it that you will not be privy to. Just as a cell in your body doesn't know the bigger human picture, it's contributing to it.

As you clear away the vestiges of the illusory self, there will be times when you feel elated as the nature and quality of your experiences heighten. There will also be periods of frustration when you sense no forward movement and occasionally what seems like a step backward, or you're going around in circles. Rather than a circle metaphor, when I experience this seeming stasis, I imagine a spiral rather than a circle. You may feel you are running around a circular track and getting nowhere, but the mere fact that you know this means that the circle is moving forward.

You know you are the observing "I", and that is an act of grace.

Cloudless Reality

Big Question Recap

Let's take another look at those big questions from the opening of the book. Here's my attempt at answering them based on what we've covered over these pages and my own life experience. Perhaps you have different answers to me; maybe no answers come to mind.

My hope in you reading this book is that I've provoked you to consider these questions, your life, and reality itself a little more deeply and with a different perspective. This is it.

> *"To see a world in a grain of sand*
> *And heaven in a wildflower,*
> *Hold infinity in the palm of your hand*
> *And eternity in an hour."*
>
> William Blake

Who Am I?

You are a part of an unfolding, conscious universe here to have experiences. You are not your body, your thoughts, or your feelings. You are the observer that is aware of those things. You are *not* a separate, individual person that is somehow incomplete. You are whole as you are; you've just lost sight of, or forgotten, who you really are.

Where Did I Come From?

There seems to be a certain teleology, or purpose, that drives the unfolding of the universe. While we cannot know the entirety of

Shall We Wrap It Up?

this telos, since we're part of it, we can intuit that there is a form of conscious intelligence driving it. Just look at the dynamism of everything, the immense creativity of it. There must be a reason why the universe is so diverse.

Since the universe is infinite, this intelligence cannot know itself completely. For it to gain any insights into its own nature, it must create "viewpoints" of itself. That is, localized forms of themselves (like whirlpools in a river) that can observe the broader landscape from their own point of view. These localized forms of consciousness are what we call life, and those forms of life that can contemplate themselves and the broader landscape, are called humans.

Why Am I Here?

You came here to experience the world according to your innate purpose. This purpose represents your role in the very unfolding of the universe. You can feel it if you look deeply enough. Finding your purpose, living a life that serves that purpose, and accumulating experiences along the way are the sole reasons you're here. You were given an amazing instrument, with the ability to think, feel, and be aware, to observe these experiences, and in doing so, contribute to the unfolding of the universe.

How Should I Live?

As far as you can, you should live your true and authentic life. Unfortunately, most of us don't know what that is or are even aware that there is such a thing. We are here to experience our lives in much the same way a tree lives as a tree or a fish lives as a fish. As a part of the universe, we are meant to live by experiencing life and reflecting on those experiences through introspection.

We have, however, misused the power of introspection. Rather than using it to keep us physically safe, we are now directed by our illusory minds to be fearful, anxious, and dissatisfied. These false beliefs obscure our authentic life and create tension between how we live and who we are. If you can live with this illusory persona and take it for what it is, you reduce its influence and start to see more of your true self. When that happens, you will live aligned with universal intention. That is a much happier life.

Where Am I Going?

Back to where you came from, a conscious universe. The experiences and insights you have accumulated throughout your life, however, are never lost. Neither is the "essence" of who you are. Everything is conserved because everything contributes to the universal unfolding. The end of life is much like waking from a dream. You merge into the universal mind, but your essence as a piece of the universe remains, just like the dream character doesn't die but is integrated into your mind and experience when you wake. This merging of your experiences and essence into the broader field of awareness adds to the evolution of the universe and, therefore, to the evolution of every conscious entity within.

> *You are a part of an unfolding, conscious universe here to have experiences. You are not your body, your thoughts, or your feelings. You are the observer that is aware of those things.*

About the Author

Pete has been an avid seeker of the truth for over twenty years. He has explored many aspects of science, spirituality, psychology, and philosophy to find the meaning of life and the world. Cloudless Reality is the culmination of years of investigation and introspection and is his first book. Pete lives in Cork, Ireland, with his wife, Fiona, their daughter, and Sadie, the pug.

www.cloudlessreality.com

Endnotes

1. |Leahy, R. *The Worry Cure: Stop Worrying and Start Living*. Piatkus Publishing, 2006.
2. Sender, R. & Milo, R. The distribution of cellular turnover in the human body. *Nat Med*. 2021;27,45–48. https://doi.org/10.1038/s41591-020-01182-9
3. What Does It Really Take to Build a New Habit? https://hbr.org/2021/02/what-does-it-really-take-to-build-a-new-habit
4. Young, E. Lifting the lid on the unconscious. New Scientist. 2018, July 25. Lifting the lid on the unconscious | New Scientist
5. Smith, J.D., Zakrzewski, A.C., Church, B.A. Formal models in animal-metacognition research: the problem of interpreting animals behavior. Psychon Bull Rev. 2016;23,1341–53. https://doi.org/10.3758/s13423-015-0985-2
6. Leahy, R. *The Worry Cure: Stop Worrying and Start Living*. Piatkus Publishing, 2006.
7. Sweetlove, L. Number of species on Earth tagged at 8.7 million. *Nature*. 2011. August 23, 2011. https://doi.org/10.1038/news.2011.498
8. Facing up to the hard question of consciousness https://royalsocietypublishing.org/doi/10.1098/rstb.2017.0342
9. Materialism Definition, Britannica. https://www.britannica.com/topic/materialism-philosophy
10. Comaford, C. Got inner peace? 5 ways to get it now. Forbes. 2012, Apr 14. https://www.forbes.com/sites/christinecomaford/2012/04/04/got-inner-peace-5-ways-to-get-it-now/
11. Chicago. Wachowski, L., and Wachowski, L. 1999. *The Matrix*. United States: Warner Bros.
12. Kastrup, B. *Why Materialism Is Baloney: How True Skeptics Know There Is No Death and Fathom Answers to Life, the Universe, and Everything*. IFF Books, 2014
13. Darwin, C. On the Origin of Species by *Means of Natural Selection*. J Murray, 1859

14 Emery, N., Markosian, N. & Sullivan, M. Time, *The Stanford Encyclopedia of Philosophy*. Winter 2020 Edition, Edward N. Zalta (ed.)

15 Capra, F. The Tao of Physics: *An Exploration of the Parallels Between Modern Physics and Eastern Mysticism*. Shambhala Publications, 2010

16 NASA/JPL-Caltech. Published 2019, Feb 5. Historical 1990, Feb 14.

17 Callen, M. & Sorek, S. Explaining the Double-Slit Experiment. *Journal of Modern Physics*. 2011; 2(1):30–5.

18 *The Observer.* Interviews with Great Scientists—Max Planck. 1931, Jan 25.

19 Britannica, The Editors of Encyclopaedia. Conservation of energy. *Encyclopedia Britannica*. 2023, Jan 13.

20 Dwoskin, H. *The Sedona Method*. Sedona Press, 2003

21 Tolle, E. *The Power of Now.* New World Library, 2004

22 Harvard Medical School. The power of the placebo effect. 2021 Dec 13.

23 National Cancer Institute. What is cancer? https://www.cancer.gov/about-cancer/understanding/what-is-cancer

24 Harvard Medical School. The power of the placebo effect. 2021 Dec 13.

25 A Preliminary Study: Efficacy of Mindfulness-Based Cognitive Therapy versus Sertraline as First-line Treatments for Major Depressive Disorder https://pubmed.ncbi.nlm.nih.gov/26085853/

26 Jeans, J. *The Mysterious Universe*. Penguin Pelican, 1937. https://www.amazon.co.uk/Mysterious-Universe-James-Jeans/dp/1163817848

27 Emoto, M. *The Hidden Messages in Water.* Atria Books, 2005.

28 Chaudhuri, H. *The Concept of Brahman in Hindu Philosophy*. *Philosophy East and West*. 1954; 4(1): 47–66. JSTOR. https://doi.org/10.2307/1396951

Bibliography

Britannica, The Editors of Encyclopaedia. Conservation of energy. *Encyclopedia Britannica*. 2023, Jan 13. https://www.britannica.com/science/conservation-of-energy

Callen, M. & Sorek, S. Explaining the Double-Slit Experiment. *Journal of Modern Physics*. 2011; 2(1):30–5. doi: 10.4236/jmp.2011.21006.

Capra, F. *The Tao of Physics: An Exploration of the Parallels between Modern Physics and Eastern Mysticism.* Shambhala Publications, 2010.

Chalmers, D. *The Character of Consciousness.* Oxford University Press, 2010.

Chaudhuri, H. The Concept of Brahman in Hindu Philosophy. *Philosophy East and West.* 1954; 4(1): 47–66. JSTOR. https://doi.org/10.2307/1396951

Comaford, C. Got inner peace? 5 ways to get it now. *Forbes.* 2012, Apr 14. https://www.forbes.com/sites/christinecomaford/2012/04/04/got-inner-peace-5-ways-to-get-it-now/

Darwin, C. *On the Origin of Species by Means of Natural Selection.* J Murray, 1859.

Dwoskin, H. *The Sedona Method.* Sedona Press, 2003

Eisendrath, S., Gillung, E., Delucchi, K., et al. A preliminary study: efficacy of mindfulness-based cognitive therapy versus sertraline as first-line treatments for major depressive disorder. *Mindfulness* (N Y). 2015 Jun 1;6(3):475–82. doi: 10.1007/s12671-014-0280-8. PMID: 26085853; PMCID: PMC4465797.

Emery, N., Markosian, N. & Sullivan, M. *Time, The Stanford Encyclopedia of Philosophy.* Winter 2020 Edition, Edward N. Zalta (ed.) https://plato.stanford.edu/archives/win2020/entries/time/

Emoto, M. *The Hidden Messages in Water.* Atria Books, 2005.

Harvard Medical School. The power of the placebo effect. 2021 Dec 13. https://www.health.harvard.edu/mental-health/the-power-of-the-placebo-effect

Jeans, J. *The Mysterious Universe.* Penguin (Pelican), 1937.

Kastrup, B. *Why Materialism Is Baloney: How True Skeptics Know There Is No Death and Fathom Answers to Life, the universe, And Everything.* IFF Books, 2014

Leahy, R. The Worry Cure: Stop Worrying and Start Living. Piatkus Publishing, 2006.

Observer, The. Interviews with Great Scientists—Max Planck. 1931, Jan 25.

Maharshi, S.R. Who Am I? Sri Ramana Asram, 1901

National Cancer Institute. What is cancer? https://www.cancer.gov/about-cancer/understanding/what-is-cancer

Palmer, C. Harnessing the power of habits. American Psychological Association. 2020 Nov 1. https://www.apa.org/monitor/2020/11/career-lab-habits

Psychology Today. Global trend: mindfulness in schools? 2019 Feb 28. https://www.psychologytoday.com/us/blog/creative-development/201902/global-trend-mindfulness-in-schools#:~:text=Countries percent20such percent20as percent20England percent20and,working percent20from percent20the percent20inside percent20out.

Ruiz, D.M. The Four Agreements. Amber-Allen Publishing. 1997

Sender, R. & Milo, R. The distribution of cellular turnover in the human body. Nat Med. 2021;27,45–48. https://doi.org/10.1038/s41591-020-01182-9

Shashkevich, A. Patient mindset matters in healing and deserves more study, experts say. News Center. Stanford Medicine. 2017, Mar 8. https://med.stanford.edu/news/all-news/2017/03/health-care-providers-should-harness-power-of-mindsets.html

Singer, M.A. The Untethered Soul: The Journey Beyond Yourself. New Harbinger Publications, U.S., 2007.

Smith, J.D., Zakrzewski, A.C., Church, B.A. Formal models in animal-metacognition research: the problem of interpreting animals behavior. Psychon Bull Rev. 2016;23,1341–53. https://doi.org/10.3758/s13423-015-0985-2

Spira, R. You Are the Happiness You Seek: Uncovering the Awareness of Being. New Harbinger, 2022

Sweetlove, L. Number of species on Earth tagged at 8.7 million. Nature. 2011. August 23, 2011. https://doi.org/10.1038/news.2011.498

Tolle, E. The Power of Now. New World Library. 2004

Young, E. Lifting the lid on the unconscious. New Scientist. 2018, July 25. Lifting the lid on the unconscious | New Scientist

Zaltman, G. How Consumers Think: Essential Insights into the Mind of the Market. Harvard Business School Press 2003.

Printed in Great Britain
by Amazon